TROMPE L'OEIL
TECHNIQUES & PROJECTS

JAN LEE JOHNSON

GUILD OF MASTER CRAFTSMAN PUBLICATIONS LTD

First published 2001 by
Guild of Master Craftsman Publications Ltd
166 High Street, Lewes, East Sussex, BN7 1XU

Text © Jan Lee Johnson 2001
© in the Work GMC Publications Ltd

Finished project photographs by Chris Skarbon
with the exception of page 34, by Anthony Bailey.
All other photographs and illustrations supplied by the author.

ISBN 1 86108 235 5

British Cataloguing in Publication Data.
A catalogue record of this book is available from the British Library.

Cover design by Yvonne Cash

Book design by Joyce Chester
Typefaces: Stone Serif and Trajan

Colour separation by Viscan Graphics Pte Ltd (Singapore)
Printed and bound by Kyodo Printing (Singapore)
under the supervision of MRM Graphics, Winslow, Buckinghamshire, UK

DEDICATION

For Thomas

ACKNOWLEDGEMENTS

I would like to thank the following for their help in creating this book:
Martin, for his invaluable contribution and patience regarding the photography;
Stephanie, warm thanks for her enthusiasm, which turned a conversation
into this book; Gill for smoothing out the text,
and the students and staff at Plymouth College of Art
and Design for their support.

ABOUT THE AUTHOR

After studying Fine Art, Jan Lee Johnson became a scenic artist for BBC Television. This involved painting a diverse range of backcloths and sets for film and television productions and a variety of painting skills from large-scale realism to portraiture and marbling.

Jan is now a lecturer at Plymouth College of Art. She is also a freelance court artist for the BBC in the West Country, providing portrait sketches at regional courts for use on television news. She has painted several public murals, most recently a 4.5m high x 30m long (15 x 100ft) trompe l'oeil painting around a stairwell for the Royal Navy at *HMS Raleigh* (see 'Gallery', page 151). Although she enjoys painting on a large scale, she is equally at home painting watercolours.

Jan's detailed trompe l'oeil paintings and artefacts, which have sold around the world, range from large panels to watercolours and painting on antique shoe trees.

CONTENTS

INTRODUCTION
to Trompe L'Oeil Painting

Trompe l'oeil (pronounced 'tromp loy') is a French phrase meaning 'to trick or fool the eye'. It is a way of painting something to momentarily convince the viewer that what he or she sees is real. This can vary from painting a flat surface to represent marble or stone, to painting distant skies to create the illusion of depth.

Painting specifically to create an illusion has been popular since ancient times. In fact the ancient Greeks enjoyed going to the theatre – where stage sets were painted to create illusions and fake

This simple design on a building in Prague creates the illusion of sharply angled stones

architecture – as early as 430BC. These Greek stage designs influenced later murals which decorated Roman interiors and expanded a room visually to create another dimension. Illusionistic murals of this type were found in the ancient city of Pompeii, in Italy – having survived the volcanic eruption of AD79 – and some can still be seen in Pompeii, while others are now preserved in museums in Rome and Naples. We know that painted illusion was important, as the murals were designed to have a 'viewpoint' in the form of a mark or disc of marble on the floor. The spectator stood on this point to view the paintings to maximum effect, and so entered into the illusion.

In Italy in the thirteenth and fourteenth centuries there was an increase in paintings simulating recesses or windows opening up imaginary spaces. Ceilings showed heavenly skies and recesses beckoned you into gardens and to contemplate far-off horizons.

During the Renaissance in Europe generally, from the fifteenth century to the end of the seventeenth century, there was a revival of Greek and Roman styles and interiors and ceilings were decorated with vast decorative and illusionistic murals. Religion was a creative driving force of illusionistic ceiling paintings and murals in the sixteenth and seventeenth centuries, too, depicting statues, figures and clouds ascending towards the infinite. The Italian illusionist tradition also took root in Austria and Bavaria, and came to England in 1671 when Antonio Verrio decorated Chatsworth House in Derbyshire and Windsor Castle, thus inspiring English painters such as William Kent who, in 1722, decorated Kensington Palace in London. The huge popularity of large-scale illusion gradually declined in the late eighteenth century in favour of more restraint, with pastel shades and simplicity reflecting the new classical style, which was called 'neoclassical'.

Close up of the decorative building exterior on page 1, showing the use of solid and broken colour

More recently, Richard Haas pioneered large-scale trompe l'oeil murals in America in the 1970s. These became popular and can be seen decorating the cities of New York, Chicago and Miami where the vast sides of blank buildings have been transformed by his painted vistas of blue sky glimpsed through decorative traditional architecture. The huge scale and the attention to detail help change and improve aspects of urban life for many city dwellers. And that is precisely what paint can do – transform otherwise blank monochrome areas, that we wouldn't give a second glance, into individual and personal spaces that give the viewer a wry smile of appreciation.

But trompe l'oeil does not need vast amounts of space in order to create an illusion. Many familiar and everyday objects can be depicted in such a way that, once painted, they take on a life of their own. The projects in this book come into that category and they are on a smaller, domestic scale. The techniques described will give you the knowledge and confidence to apply paint to create a range of illusionistic textures – such as stone, marble and mosaic pattern – on flat surfaces, and the outlines and templates will make it easier for you to paint three-dimensional objects. There is advice on how to block in simple shapes, mix colours and use glazes to achieve a realistic effect, and guidance and useful tips each step of the way.

You don't need to be a trained artist to follow the techniques and projects in this collection, nor will you need to spend a fortune on paints and other materials. I show you how to accomplish something you can be proud of and will enjoy creating and, equipped with this information, you will be able to modify my trompe l'oeil designs to create an individual and personal style to suit yourself and your surroundings.

Materials, Equipment and Paint Effects

MATERIALS, EQUIPMENT AND PAINT EFFECTS

The following materials and equipment are used for the projects in this book, but each project has its own list of specific items needed.

MDF

I have chosen **MDF** (medium density fibreboard) for some of the projects, because it is light, inexpensive, easily cut to the desired size and is readily available in DIY stores. Once cut, I recommend asking a woodworker to shape the edges with a router, because it makes the items look more attractive, and gives them a professionally-finished look so they don't require framing.

WOOD PANELS

Other projects have been painted on **wood panels**, which kitchen suppliers sell as panels for cupboard doors. These are generally very well made from good quality wood, come in all shapes and sizes and are also inexpensive. I particularly like to use the 'frame'

Non-clogging finishing paper

around the centre panel and enjoy finding imaginative ways of using the 'real' edge against a trompe l'oeil painted edge to trick the observer's eye.

PRIMER

New surfaces of wood or MDF are, usually, ready to paint with a **white acrylic primer** but, if varnished, must be thoroughly sanded to remove the varnish before priming. It is best to use a good quality primer and not to thin the paint, as this would inhibit coverage. Once the paint is dry, sand before applying a further coat.

SANDPAPER

Sanding between coats will remove telltale brush marks and any drips that may have occurred. A medium '**non-clogging finishing paper**', which is recommended for use with paints and varnishes, should be used throughout the projects.

BRUSHES

Sable brushes in sizes 1, 2, and 3 are essential for detailed work. Although more expensive, they outlive nylon brushes and have a far better 'tip' with which to paint detail. Use **nylon** or **bristle brushes**, either flat or round in sizes 5, 6, 7 and 8 for general painting. Larger brushes for blocking in bigger areas should be 25mm and 50mm (1in and 2in) and of good quality, especially when applying varnish, so buy artists' quality brushes. A **badger softener**, a brush with very soft natural bristles, is used to produce a marbled effect, graining and for general blending by 'tickling' the surface with the tips of the bristles. A **graining brush** has long bristles and produces patterns simulating the grain of wood. An **oblong stippling brush** (100 x 25mm/4 x 1in), with very firm bristles, evens out brush marks by producing a fine stippled effect. It is very useful for blending colours, and for shading, by subtly spreading darker areas onto lighter areas and vice versa.

THE MARKS BRUSHES CAN MAKE

Stippling brush

Stippled stencil design

Oblong stippling brush

Nylon brush (15mm/⅝in)

Household brush (38mm/1½in)

Bristle brush (size 8)

Round bristle brush (size 12)

Round nylon brush (size 4)

Round sable brush (size 1)

Graining brush

COLOURS USED THROUGHOUT THIS BOOK

raw umber

monestial green

burnt umber

ultramarine blue

raw sienna

cobalt blue

yellow ochre

cadmium red

cadmium yellow

purple

Brushes from left: sable size 3; nylon flat x 2; round stippling brush; flat 50mm (2in) for varnishing; badger softener; grainer; long stippling brush; three sizes of bristle

ACRYLIC PAINT

I have used **artists' quality acrylic paints** for all the projects. Firstly because acrylics are water soluble, so the brushes wash out in water. Secondly because they are very versatile – the paint can be used thickly straight from the tube as well as in transparent washes, like watercolour. Thirdly, they dry quite quickly and are therefore controllable.

Acrylics are available in pots and handy-sized tubes: tubes are easier to use and contain adequate paint for the projects in this book, but pots are more cost-effective in the long term. I have used an extensive colour range for these projects, including rich earth colours and vivid primary colours, all mixed from the following ten paints, together with black and white:

raw umber
burnt umber
raw sienna
yellow ochre
cadmium yellow
monestial green
ultramarine blue
cobalt blue
cadmium red
purple

SCUMBLE GLAZE

I recommend mixing **acrylic scumble glaze** (which is available from art and craft shops) with acrylics, because it is specially formulated to prevent the paint from drying out too quickly and it also adds translucency. Keep a teaspoon-size dollop of scumble glaze on the side of your palette and dip the paintbrush into this each time you are mixing the

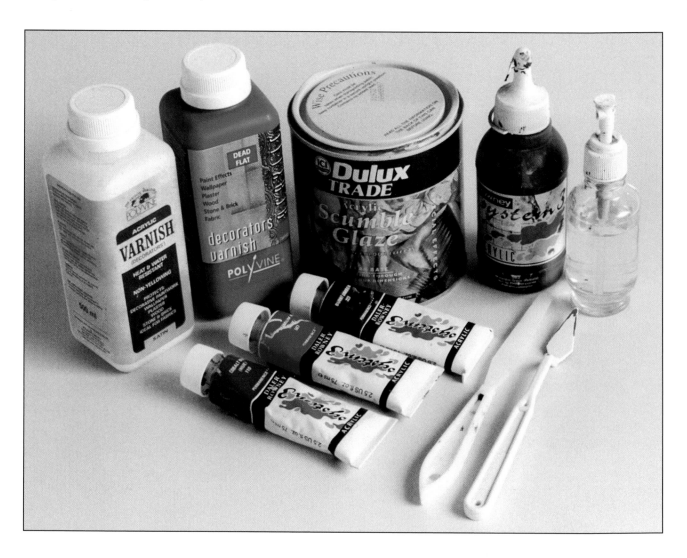

paint for decorative effects; replenish the dollop as necessary.

Scumble is also used to make glazes which are used, for example, when creating marbled effects. One part scumble is mixed with three parts paint to create a transparent, coloured glaze which allows the preceding colour or base coat to show through.

SPRAY DIFFUSER

A **spray diffuser**, containing water, is useful for keeping paints moist while working.

VARNISH

This should be water-based. I have used 'Polyvine' **acrylic varnish** – which is widely available from art shops – to protect the finishes. 'Dead Flat' varnish protects the surface with a clear matt finish, while the 'Satin' gives a subtle sheen.

Varnishes, scumble glaze, acrylic paints, spray diffuser and plastic palette knives

ROLLERS

Small foam rollers (50mm/2in sleeve) are very cheap and, when using masking tape, are ideal for neat blocking in; they are also useful when stencilling, or for painting on a rough surface such as an outdoor wall. **Larger foam rollers** (125mm/5in sleeve) should be used when you need to block in bigger areas.

When you need to produce quick and easy textural effects, which can be applied to any area, you can simply adapt a foam roller 'sleeve' by pulling out small, random pieces of foam with your fingers. Vary the size of the holes and don't forget to pull pieces out at the ends of your rollers as well, to avoid a straight line (see facing page).

CREATING TEXTURE WITH A CUSTOMIZED FOAM ROLLER

Foam roller before customizing

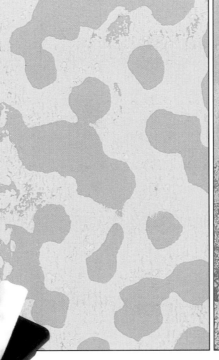

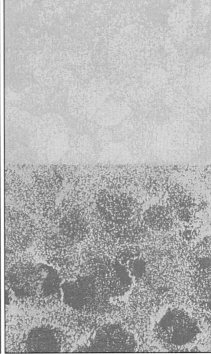

*Small pieces
of foam taken out,
to add more texture*

Effect achieved with a customized foam roller

Use a paint tray to roll out the paint evenly before applying, and be sure to overlap the last area with your next rollered area to create an even coverage. I used this quick and efficient method to produce stone textures for the external fresco (Project 9, page 98).

Fluffy or **'sheepskin' rollers** can create more even texture very quickly on a surface, and are very easily cleaned by removing the 'sleeve' from the handle.

Natural sponges in a range of sizes are invaluable for creating a variety of textures on all types of surface and **foam applicators** are useful for applying paint to stencils.

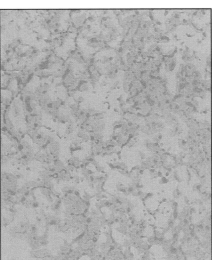

Fluffy or sheepskin roller   *Natural sponge*   *Natural sponge*

EFFECTS ACHIEVED WITH A GRAINING COMB

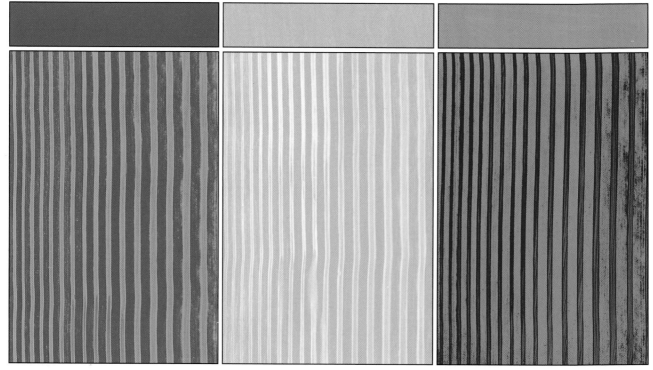

Yellow paint over a varnished green base coat	*White paint over varnished pale blue base coat*	*Dark blue over a varnished pink base coat*

EFFECTS ACHIEVED WITH A GRAINING ROCKER

Yellow paint over a varnished green base coat	*White paint over varnished pale blue base coat*	*Dark blue over a varnished pink base coat*

Left to right: rubber graining rocker; natural sponge; rubber graining comb; small foam roller; two foam applicators; small sponge

Effect achieved by combining the graining comb and rocker

GRAINING ROCKERS AND COMBS

Two rubber tools for producing the effect of wood grain are a **graining rocker** and a **graining comb**. The principle is the same for both these tools: they are used over a base coat (existing white or a painted

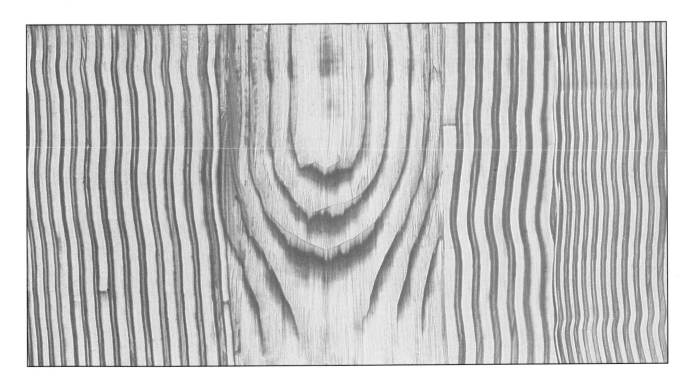

colour) which has been varnished to make a smooth surface for the tool to glide over. Acrylic paint – watered down to the consistency of single cream – is then brushed over the dry varnish with a household paintbrush, and the graining comb or rocker applied to achieve the desired effect.

The **graining comb** has thick and thin teeth which create varying widths of line when the comb is pulled through the wet paint to reveal the base coat. It is useful for purely decorative effects as well.

The **graining rocker** is pulled through the wet paint with a smooth action, and rocked every now and again to produce an effect which simulates the heart of the wood.

For a more realistic effect, you can alternate stripes made with the graining comb with the curved 'heart grain' produced by the rocker. But don't over use the rocker – the 'heart wood' effect has more impact and realism when used sparingly: one strip of 'wood' with rocker between two or three of straight grain looks more convincing.

> ### TIP
> ———
> *Mix the paint with scumble glaze, to make the action smoother and stop the paint drying out too quickly. This will give you time to wipe off the paint if you make a mistake.*

RULING LINES

A selection of **rulers** is essential for marking out, cutting and measuring and clear plastic rulers, of various sizes, are particularly helpful. A **T-square ruler** is very useful for measuring accurate and level lines and invaluable for the tile table (Project 4) and stone window (Project 6), as the edge of the 'T' ensures that straight horizontal and vertical lines can be measured.

MASKING TAPE

Masking tape is a great time saver if you use it to mask off areas where you want to paint a neat edge quickly and easily. I recommend using '**Scotch Magic™ Tape**' for surfaces where a fine finish is all important – the celebration tray for example, in Project 3. When used on dry surfaces it becomes

almost invisible once in place, but the major advantage is that paint doesn't 'bleed' underneath (unless it is thinned far too much with water) and the tape can be removed easily after painting, once the paint is dry.

CUTTING MAT

I recommend using a **self-healing cutting mat** for safety. These are non-slip, protect your work surface, and the flexible surface of the rubber mat is ideal when cutting stencil designs.

CRAFT KNIVES

I use disposable **craft knives** which stay sharp for a reasonably long time; those I use have plastic handles and a replaceable safety blade cover.

SPIRIT LEVEL

A spirit level is useful for marking horizontal lines on a vertical surface (e.g. the fresco in Project 9). They are widely available, but it is easy to make your own and instructions are given on the facing page.

CARBON PAPER

I recommend **non-wax carbon paper**. Used underneath a tracing, it transfers the image to the surface to be painted and the outline can be removed

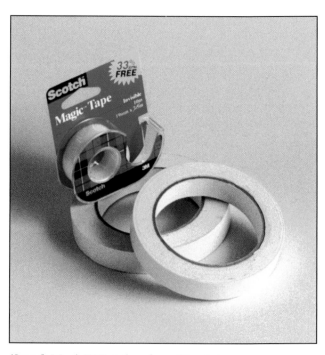

'Scotch Magic™ Tape' and masking tape

with a pencil rubber. It is sold by craft shops in sets of six grey sheets, and is also available in a pack of various colours, which means a blue surface can have red or yellow traced lines for a more visible contrast. The sheets are reusable for several tracings.

Tracing paper and carbon paper

MAKING YOUR OWN SPIRIT LEVEL

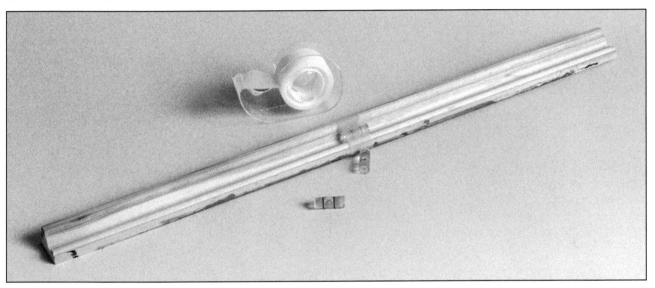

A home-made spirit level

It is easy to make a spirit level which is lighter and simpler to use than a shop-bought one. To make your own, buy a 1m (3ft) length of wood moulding and a small cheap spirit level from a hardware shop. Remove the 'bubble' from the spirit level, place it in the centre of your length of wood (the curved moulding will help to hold the 'bubble') and fix it in place with clear tape.

To use, adjust the angle of the spirit level until the bubble is centred, then pencil an accurate and level line across. With practice, accurate painted lines can also be produced by resting the metal part of the loaded brush against the length of wood, and pulling downwards for a vertical line, or pulling across from one side to another for a horizontal line.

TROMPE L'OEIL TECHNIQUES

The following techniques will help you to follow
the projects convincingly.

LACE EFFECT

1 Paint your chosen surface with an **eau de nil** base coat (mixed from **white**, **monestial green**, a little **ultramarine blue** and a very little **raw umber** to mellow the shade). Allow to dry, then trace the design from the template, and transfer to the painted surface, using carbon paper.

3 Mix half a teaspoon **monestial green** with a quarter teaspoon of **raw umber** and a quarter teaspoon of **scumble glaze**. Thin with water and, using a **size 1 sable brush**, paint underneath and below the lace edges with this shadow mix.

2 Mix one teaspoon **white** with a quarter teaspoon of **yellow ochre**, thin with water and, using a **size 1 sable brush**, fill in the delicate lace shape with this cream paint. Use a **size 3 brush** for the larger areas.

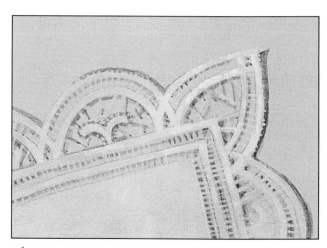

4 Build up the lacy effect by adding the tiny connecting threads, using a **size 1 brush** and the basic cream paint. Finally, for a very authentic look, paint tiny blobs on the edge of the lace, using the very tip of the brush.

MARBLING AND VEINING

1 Paint a cream base coat on your chosen surface, allow the paint to dry, then apply a coat of satin varnish. Once the varnish is dry, mix a quarter teaspoon of raw umber with a teaspoon of scumble glaze and apply this mixture with a stippling brush, working in a diagonal section.

3 As soon as you have painted a vein, work over it with a **badger brush**, in several directions, to break up and soften the line and imitate the veining found on real marble. Continue until you've built up a network of veins that sometimes cross over each other, but don't overdo it or do too many. (See 'Tip' below.)

2 Use a **size 1 sable brush** to apply the veins. Darken the basic mix with more **raw umber**, or **black** for a darker variation. Dip the brush in the glaze and, holding the handle end loosely between thumb and finger, roll the brush as you pull it towards you in a diagonal direction, to produce veining lines of varying widths. Be careful not to let the paint dry before the next stage.

4 When veining is complete, make a white glaze with half a teaspoonful of **white paint**, half a teaspoonful of **scumble glaze** and water to thin. Apply this with a **stippling brush**, in a stabbing action, and then soften with a **badger brush**. When dry, use a **fine sandpaper** to remove any blobs and to generally smooth the surface before applying **satin varnish**.

TIP

Wash the badger brush out with water straight after use, as acrylic paint dries quickly on this type of brush and the ends can get clogged with paint.

GRISAILLE

Grisaille (which derives from the French word 'gris', meaning grey) is a technique of monochromatic painting, originally all in shades of grey. In the seventeenth century this was a popular method of painting imitation panelling and low reliefs, and especially imitation statues. In a modern interpretation, you can use different colours in the same way to great effect. To illustrate this, I have taken a standard 10 x 15cm (4 x 6in) modern school photograph and given it an 'antique' look, by interpreting it in sepia tones. All quantities given are for this size but, whatever image you choose, you can adjust quantities and apply the guidelines given here. (See also pages 46–7.)

1 Prepare the surface to be painted with a base coat of pale **raw umber**, made from one teaspoon of **white acrylic** and a quarter teaspoon of raw umber. Leave to dry. Photocopy your image to the desired size, trace and transfer to your painted surface (see page 124).

2 Use a translucent glaze for the darker areas, mixed from one teaspoon of **raw umber**, half a teaspoon of **scumble glaze** and water to dilute. Paint on this colour with a **size 1 sable brush**, aiming to build up the various sepia tones gradually.

3 Use the same brush and colour to add the finer details, in this case on the face. Carefully define the eyes, the shadow under the nose, the mouth, the outline of the face and the outline of the jacket collar and stripes on the tie. Work outwards from the outline of the face, using the brush in several directions to suggest a textured background, then paint the oval frame with neat **raw umber**, thinned with water.

4 For the flesh colour on the face, use leftover base coat – either darkened with **raw umber** or lightened with **white** – and add a touch of scumble glaze for translucency. Follow the different tones of your photograph and note their variations as you match them with tones of **raw umber** and **white**.

Paint the eyes with the very tip of the brush, using **raw umber** thinned with **scumble glaze** and, if you like, strengthen the colour with a touch of **black**. Paint the shirt with **white acrylic** and use the end of a **cocktail stick** to put in the tiny highlights in the eyes. As a final touch, to give immediate life to the portrait, add **white** highlights on the cheeks, end of the nose and bottom lip.

I have used artistic licence here, combining the head in the photograph on the facing page with the body in this photograph

CREATING FAUX LIMESTONE

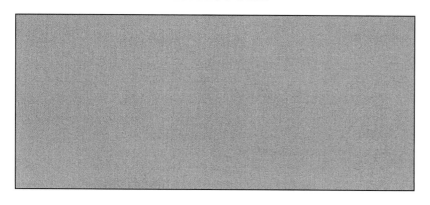

1 Mix a tablespoon of **white acrylic** with half a teaspoon of **raw umber** acrylic and thin to a creamy consistency with water. Paint the plaque with this mixture, using a **25mm (1in) brush**, then leave this base coat to dry.

2 Measure half a teaspoon of **raw umber** and thin to a milky consistency with water and **scumble glaze**, then add a quarter of a teaspoon of **white paint** to lighten it. Press this colour onto the base coat with a **damp sponge**, to replicate the crumbly broken texture of limestone.

3 Next, thin some **white paint** to a milky consistency with water and **scumble glaze**. Press this lightly into the surface with a damp sponge, to simulate the chalky appearance of limestone.

4 To create the characteristic tiny flecks on the surface, mix a **mid-grey colour**, add a little **raw umber** to darken slightly, then thin with water to a milky consistency and add a little **scumble glaze**. You should have about a tablespoonful of paint when thinned. Protect the surrounding surfaces with **newspaper**, then dip an **old toothbrush** in the paint. Point it at the surface to be covered, brush side up, and pull your thumb along the bristles towards you, to splatter random flecks of paint. (N.B. If you push, rather than pull, your thumb through the bristles, *you* will end up covered in paint!) Position the brush a few inches from the surface for larger flecks and further away for finer flecks. Leave to dry, then apply **matt varnish**.

CREATING FAUX SANDSTONE

1 Mix one tablespoon of **white acrylic** with a quarter teaspoon of **yellow ochre** and thin to a creamy consistency with water. Apply to the surface with a **25mm (1in) brush** and leave to dry.

2 Mix half a teaspoon of **yellow ochre** with a quarter teaspoon each of **raw sienna** and **raw umber**, and thin to a milky consistency with water and **scumble glaze**. This combination produces quite a 'hot' colour – if you prefer a 'cooler' colour, add a little **grey**. Sponge (or stipple) this mixture lightly onto the surface with a **damp sponge** – leaving broken areas of the paler base coat visible – until you have achieved an overall sandstone texture.

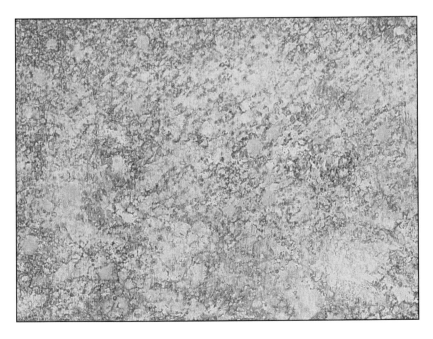

3 If you need to expose more of the base coat, press a clean damp sponge into the surface to remove more of the darker toned colour. Once you are happy with the result, leave to dry, then apply **matt varnish**.

N.B. Quantities given are for an area approximately 36 x 23cm (14 x 9in), the same size as Project 1, the wall plaque. Apply to surface previously painted with two coats of acrylic primer. If using faux limestone or faux sandstone as an alternative to the faux granite specified for the wall plaque, follow the project from stage 6 onwards (see page 30) for further decoration.

CREATING CRACKS IN STONEWORK

1 Paint a **cream base coat** onto your chosen surface and leave it to dry. Mix some diluted **grey paint** with **scumble glaze** and **sponge** over the whole surface, as the basic stone colour.

Once this is dry, mark out horizontal and vertical lines with a **pencil and ruler**, to define the area of each stone block. First paint the horizontal lines: mix some **black** and **raw umber** with a little **scumble glaze** and, resting the metal part of a **size 3** or **4 round nylon brush** on a **straight-edge**, paint an even line for the shadow. Next, paint in the shorter vertical dark lines that form the ends of the blocks.

2 Tint some **white** with **raw umber** to make an off-white for the highlighted top edge of the stone blocks. Paint these underneath the dark shadow lines, butting them up to the edge. When the horizontal lines are completed, paint in the shorter vertical edges as before, to make an even and regular line. Continue until all the stone blocks have shadow and highlights.

To create the cracks in the stone, mix some **raw umber** with scumble glaze, thin with water, and use this mix to paint random lines and blobs across the stones. To complete the trompe l'oeil effect, add some touches of white.

PAINTING SOLID OBJECTS WITH SHADOWS AND HIGHLIGHTS

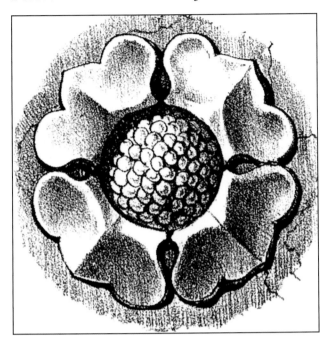

1 Undercoat your chosen surface with **cream paint**. **Varnish**, then leave to dry. Sponge with a mixture of diluted **raw umber**, with a touch of **scumble glaze**, and leave to dry.

2 Trace the basic shape (above) and transfer to your surface by pencilling through **carbon paper**.

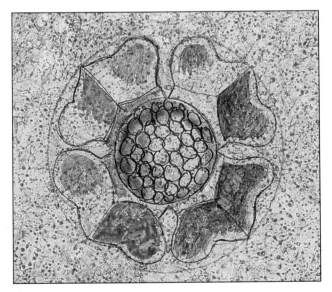

4 Add more **raw umber** to the paint and build up the shadowed areas as shown. Paint neat sharp lines along dividing lines of each stone petal, blending downwards to the edges. Outline the shape along the bottom and right. The centre circle of pods is defined with darker paint around the right-hand side. Following the pencil line, outline each pod in the centre circle.

3 Mix some **raw umber** and **scumble glaze** and, with a **size 1 brush**, paint in the shadows as illustrated, blending out towards the edges and concentrating the shadows on the bottom and right-hand side.

5 Define the highlights on each pod as shown, using pure **white acrylic** on the tip of the brush, and painting along the ridges of each stone petal. Darken each petal by using a touch of **black** with the **raw umber** and blending the colour outwards towards the edges. You can give more character to the surrounding stone effect, and added texture to the sculpture, by mixing a shade of **raw umber** darker than the sponged colour (i.e. more paint to **scumble glaze**) and painting this around the carved rosette.

CREATING WOODEN PLANKING

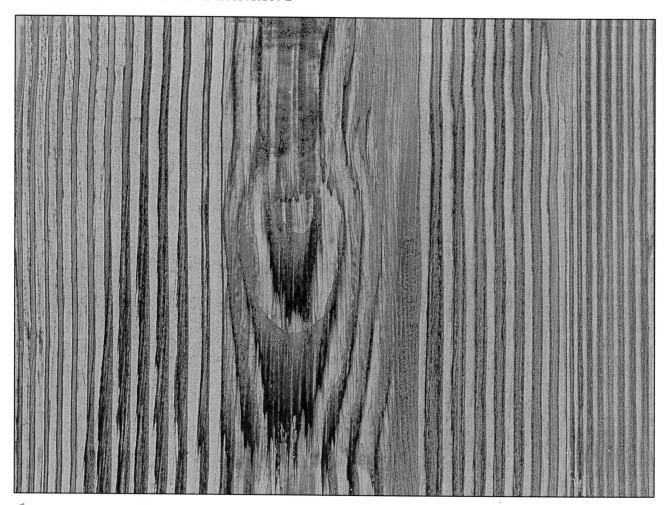

1 First prepare a grey-green base coat. Mix one tablespoon of **white paint**, a quarter teaspoon of **monestial green** and a quarter teaspoon of **black paint** and brush this mixture onto your surface. Leave to dry, then apply one coat of **satin varnish**.

2 Once the varnish is dry, mix the dark green combing colour from one teaspoon of **monestial green**, a quarter teaspoon of **black** and a half teaspoon of **scumble glaze**. Thin with water, aiming for the consistency of thin cream. Paint this over the varnished base coat with a **household paintbrush**, covering an area of 20cm (8in) or so, the width of two 'pullings' of the **graining comb** or **rocker**.

3 Start with the **graining comb**. First, make sure the surface you are working on is firmly anchored, so that it doesn't slip during the process. Hold the comb with both hands – with thumbs on either side – and, starting

on the left, pull the comb down through the paint, from top to bottom. The comb should glide through very easily, because of the varnish underneath, but remember, the lines don't have to be dead straight to be convincing, as the natural grain of wood always undulates slightly.

4 After completing a length of combing, take a **household paintbrush** and paint in another strip, painting up to, and slightly overlapping, the grained edge so that there are no gaps. Next use the **rocker** – pulling it down from top to bottom in the same way – but rocking gently back and forth as you do so, to give the characteristic look of the heart wood.

5 Now start again with your **graining comb**, overlapping the previously grained paint slightly as you go. Continue working in the same way, until the whole area is completed, then leave to dry.

6 Mix a glaze of a half teaspoon of **monestial green**, quarter teaspoon of **raw umber** and one teaspoon of **scumble glaze**, thin with water and apply with a **graining brush**, in a downwards motion, over the whole area. The bristles will make finer brush lines which fill in the broader combed lines, adding realism, and the green-brown glaze tones the existing colours into a more harmonious and unifying tone. Leave to dry.

7 For the dark shadow, which forms the edge of a plank, measure 10cm (4in) widths of planking and draw a pencil line from top to bottom, to use as a guide. Load a **size 3** or **4 nylon round brush** with a mixture of **black** and **raw umber**, thinned with water to a milky consistency. Position **a length of moulding** vertically, next to the pencil line and, resting the metal part of the brush against this, pull the brush down in an even and smooth action. The glazed surface will help the brush to glide down.

8 When all the edges of the planking are painted in this way, add in the highlights to complete the effect: for these, make a mixture of **white**, tone down slightly with **monestial green**, and thin with water to a milky consistency. Paint the highlights adjacent to the shadow, using the **moulding** as a guide, and a **size 3** or **4 brush and following the same procedure** as in the previous stage.

PRACTICALITIES

on't underestimate the time it will take you to achieve the desired effects. It is worth spending time and effort to get it right, and important to prepare surfaces properly and allow paint and varnish to dry thoroughly between coats.

Before you start on an actual project, practise the techniques on offcuts of wood or a wall that you intend to paint over – experimenting before you begin on the real thing will build up your confidence and help you to achieve convincing results. Shadows, highlights and perspective, for instance, are needed for most of the projects, so note where the light source is coming from, as this will determine the position of the shadows of any objects you choose to paint. It is also a good idea to study the highlights and shadows of other objects in the area where the subject is to be hung or painted.

Where the projects call for perspective it is explained simply with diagrams, is uncomplicated and does not dominate the design (see diagrams below). Only a basic understanding of perspective is needed to create a three-dimensional effect on a flat surface: just remember that all parallel lines recede, and appear to converge on the horizon at a point called the vanishing point. (See Project 10, page 106.)

Think about your location. Techniques for creating faux (false) stone form the basis of many trompe l'oeil effects. I have created a granite effect in the first project because that stone is dominant in southwest England where I live. What dominates in

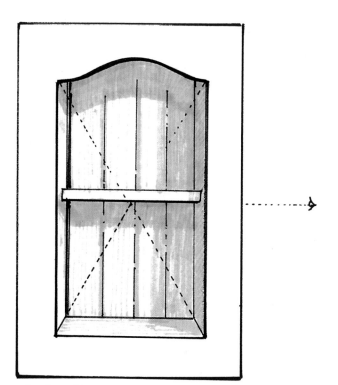

The dotted line indicates the vanishing point

Applying perspective to indicate an open window

your locality? Look at the samples I have painted and see how different stone effects can be created by stippling different paint colours

Once you have transformed a flat surface into fake stone or marble, the templates and instructions will help you add the extra painted trompe l'oeil details to create startlingly realistic effects. Then, when you have completed a small project, your ability and confidence will increase to consider a larger project. The trompe l'oeil stone window might be your next choice, having mastered faux stone. Painting highlights on a stone finish to create a rounded 'carved' effect becomes simpler when the stages are explained. Using restrained colours to paint an illusion of distance, your window with a 'view' can be positioned in your home for maximum effect.

If you want to modify the designs, to create an individual and personal style to suit yourself and your surroundings, start simply. You might want to include favourite ornaments, such as a vase or plate in a trompe l'oeil cupboard design, and then place them nearby to extend the visual trickery. Look at magazines and books for detailed photographs of images that can be used as reference – an ornament or butterfly, for instance. When you have gathered the objects that you wish to paint, make outlines of each shape on a separate sheet of tracing paper. These can then be enlarged to the appropriate size on a photocopier, and a stencil made (see pages 124–5).

Once you have tried out the smaller projects, you might like to exercise your skills on a larger-scale project such as the life-size mural (see page 106). If you prefer, you could use the dimensions

Creating false stone forms the basis of many trompe l'oeil effects. Here, faux stone is painted on a wooden mirror frame and embellished with insects and leaves

of a window in your home as a reference. The overall size is not daunting, provided you remember that it is broken down into sections.

Whichever project you choose, you will find the techniques are thoroughly explained, with useful tips and hints at every stage. But remember, it is important to read your chosen project through carefully before you begin, to ensure that you have everything to hand. Armed with this information your trompe l'oeil painting can develop gradually, at your own pace, and you can be sure of a stunning result.

FAUX STONE WALL PLAQUE

with trompe l'oeil painted panel, ivy leaves and butterfly

This attractive project includes a step by step guide to creating a faux stone finish, which enables you to create a very good imitation in just a few hours. The finish described here is 'granite' but, if you prefer, follow the instructions for 'limestone' or 'sandstone' on pages 18 and 19.

Faux limestone plaque

Faux sandstone plaque

 Templates for plaque bevel, ivy and butterfly on page 126, numbers on page 127.

MATERIALS AND EQUIPMENT

Plaque, approx. 36cm wide x 23cm high (14 x 9in), shop-bought or made

White acrylic primer

Sandpaper: medium grade, non-clogging finishing paper

A good quality household paintbrush, 25mm (1in)

Sable artists' brushes, sizes 2, 3 and 4

Stippling brush

Acrylic paints: black; white; raw umber; ultramarine blue; purple; monestial green; cadmium yellow; raw sienna; cadmium red

Two natural sponges, each the size of the palm of your hand

Scumble glaze

Spray diffuser

Narrow length of wood or moulding (see page 30, step 3)

Ruler

Pencil and rubber

Tracing paper

Non-wax carbon paper

Chinagraph pencil

Transparent masking tape (Scotch Magic™ Tape)

Stencil card (or transparent Fablon, if making your own stencil)

Round stencil brush (100 x 25mm/4 x 1in)

Craft knife

Cutting mat

Acrylic varnish ('dead flat' or matt)

Templates are included for the plaque and panel, numbers – with areas of light and shadow indicated – ivy and a decorative butterfly, with dotted outlines for cast shadow. If you are not a woodworker, the basic plaque shape can be bought from a craft shop. They are sold as 'blanks' for decorating, and are either unvarnished wood or MDF, with routed edges.

Good quality household brushes are adequate for applying the base coats of paint, but artists' brushes will be needed for detail and the finer work. Use a non-wax carbon paper when tracing, so the outlines can be removed with a pencil rubber once the painting is complete.

THE BASIC PLAQUE

If the plaque shape is being made, photocopy the corner templates onto tracing paper, then place the carbon paper between the tracing paper and the MDF; trace the outlines of the four corner shapes onto the MDF, to form the plaque outline. It is then a simple procedure for a woodworker to cut out the shape and create the carved edge with a router.

2 Mix a mid-grey colour with a tablespoon of white acrylic and half a teaspoon of black acrylic, then add a little raw umber, to make a warm grey colour. Thin to a creamy consistency then apply over the primer with the household brush. Leave to dry for fifteen minutes or so.

3 Mix a darker shade of grey paint by adding a touch of black, blue and purple, to create a richer shade of dark grey. Thin with water to a milky consistency, and apply with a stippling brush in a stabbing action, to replicate the texture of granite. Have a dollop of scumble glaze next to your colours and dab the brush into this as you replenish the colours – the scumble glaze will add transparency and reveal the paler base coat underneath. Continue with the next stage before the paint dries.

1 THE 'GRANITE' BASE
Once you have the basic plaque shape, apply a first coat of acrylic primer to the front and sides of the plaque using an ordinary household paintbrush. Try to brush out the paint on the surface, to prevent telltale brush strokes. Leave to dry, sand down, then apply a second coat. If necessary, sand down again.

4 Now take a small amount of blue and purple acrylic – about 12mm (½in) of each, if squeezed from a tube – and place them separately on your plate or palette. Apply these colours to the still-wet stippled surface, stabbing with the stippling brush and dabbing with a squeezed out

damp sponge alternately, to vary the size of texture. Put a half teaspoon of white acrylic on your palette and apply this with a clean damp sponge to create lighter broken shades of grey, with random flecks of blue, purple and white. Make sure you apply the texture evenly and coat the edges all round, then dab with a clean squeezed-out sponge to soak up any excess paint.

5 After five minutes or so, spray some water droplets onto the painted surface with a diffuser, wait for a minute or two, then gently dab the droplets with a clean damp sponge to reveal dappled areas of base coat. Don't overwork the surface: the aim is to add depth and character as the surface takes on the look of stone.

The faux granite is now complete. Leave it to dry, then apply a 'dead flat' varnish.

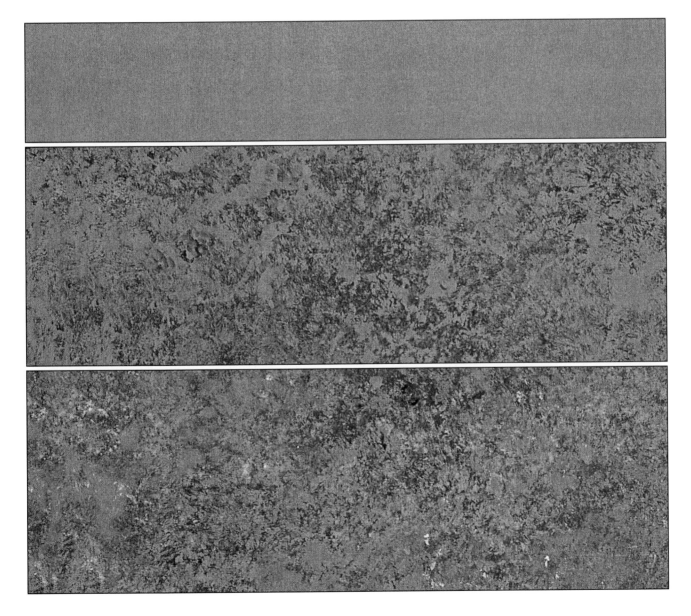

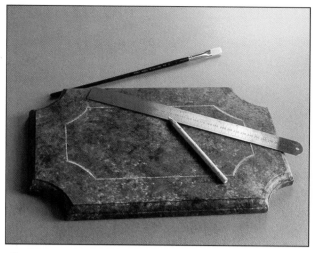

1 THE TROMPE L'OEIL BEVEL

Once the varnish is dry, draw on lines to indicate the inset 'bevel', using a white chinagraph pencil and ruler. The dotted line on the corner template (see page 126) can be used for guidance.

3

Load a size 4 flat bristle brush with paint and, using your strip of wood as a steadying guide, paint in the dark shadows: the metal part of the brush should be touching the wood as it is pulled along. As the plaque has been varnished, the brush should glide over the surface.

2

Divide the drawn shape into two distinct areas, to indicate where to paint shadow and highlight for the trompe l'oeil bevel, and separate these with masking tape.

For the shadowed area squeeze equal amounts of black and raw umber (12mm/½in or so) and add a touch of purple for richness of colour. Mix, then thin to a milky consistency with water.

4

Follow the same procedure for the highlights on the remaining half, painting them with white, which has been thinned slightly.

TIP
—

Avoid thick paint when painting in shadows, as the stone surface should just be visible. Thinned paint gives colour without density.

TIP
—

For a neat dividing line between the shadow and highlight, place a strip of masking tape along the centre (where dark meets light) – this will reveal a neat painted edge when removed.

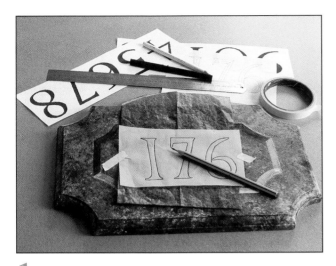

1 THE NUMBERS AND LEAVES

Next, trace your chosen numbers from the template on page 127, enlarging or reducing them if necessary. Fix the tracing in position with masking tape, then slide carbon paper underneath. Retrace the lines using a sharp pencil, indicating the division lines for shadows and highlights.

2 Next paint the numbers, taking care to keep the dark and light areas of each numeral consistent: the left side should be in shadow and the right side showing highlights – if in doubt, refer to the template. Start with the shadows, masking off the highlighted areas with Magic Tape, to ensure a crisp dividing line between the shadows and highlights. Mix raw umber and black, and dilute with water to a thin cream consistency, but not so the paint 'runs' off the brush. Paint in the shadows of each numeral with this mixture, using a size 3 artists' brush.

3 Once the shadow paint is completely dry, remove the masking tape and reposition fresh tape over the newly-painted shadowed areas. Paint in the highlights in the same way, using some white acrylic, thinned to the same consistency as the shadow paint.

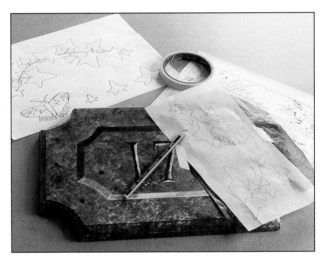

4 Trace the ivy leaf design from the template on page 126 then, if necessary, use a photocopier to enlarge it to the required size. Position the tracing carefully on the plaque, tape into place, then slide carbon paper underneath and retrace the design firmly.

5 Make a stencil of the ivy leaves. Either trace the design onto stencil card, or cover both sides of the photocopied template in clear Fablon (see pages 124–5). Cut out the leaves to reveal the stencil.

6 Now mix the paint for the leaf colour, blending and varying the shades of green for each leaf. Use monestial green and cadmium yellow, darkening with a touch of black or raw umber, and brightening with more yellow and a touch of white. Position the stencils over their corresponding drawn leaves, using masking tape to secure them, and stipple on the paint with a stippling brush.

7 Remove the stencil, and use an artists' brush to finish off the leaves and to paint the stems.

1 **THE BUTTERFLY**

A butterfly positioned on the plaque will add interest and colour and, with painted shadows, will enhance the trompe l'oeil effect. Transfer the butterfly design on page 126 from the template to the plaque, as in stage 1, page 31.

2 Then, using a sable artists' brush and a bright colour – I used cadmium yellow with a small amount of white – carefully fill in the outline.

3 Make a stencil of the butterfly from the same template, and apply your chosen colours through this using a small stencil brush or a firm bristle brush. You can apply several colours, blending them as you go, as the stencil will ensure a neat outline.

I used a butterfly guide to get accurate detail for my 'Painted Lady' butterfly, but you may want to include a species familiar to you or your area.

4 Use the template again as a guide for pencilling in the outline for the shadow cast by the butterfly and the ivy leaves.

5 Mix the shadow colour from a little black and raw umber paint and thin with water to make a cream consistency. Vary the colour if you want, by adding purple or ultramarine blue to add richness, and less or more water for intensity. Apply with a fine artists' brush, working from the edges of the butterflies and leaves, out towards the pencilled outlines. It is this final addition of shadow that gives an impression of three dimensions, that all important trick of the eye – the illusion of reality.

6 Once the paint is dry, apply a coat of varnish and your plaque is complete.

MOSAIC-EFFECT TOILET SEAT

with Greek urn and shell designs

True mosaic consists of small pieces of cut stone (called 'tesserae') embedded in plaster – an art first used to decorate rooms in Ancient Greece. It became a very popular medium and reached its height in early Christian Art, when mosaic was used to create a surface decoration of beautiful and colourful works of art, with the tesserae shape, size and colour varying according to the design being represented.

This project is for a trompe l'oeil 'mosaic' toilet seat for a modern bathroom. It uses a design of a classical-style Greek urn but, instead of cutting up pieces of stone and mixing plaster, 'tesserae' are made from small cubes of foam rubber. These are dipped into acrylic paint and the 'mosaic' is printed by pressing down the cube on the surface to be covered. In a short time this very effective and flexible process can transform an area, making it look surprisingly like a genuine mosaic at a fraction of the cost; it can be completed in a day or two, so it is a lot quicker, too.

Wooden toilet seats are the ideal surface for the beginner to decorate as they are a manageable size and can be used to create an unusual hand-painted feature to complement the colour scheme in a bathroom. They are sold in DIY shops, in standard sizes to fit most bathrooms and are available in unvarnished wood. They are ready to paint and do not need any preparation, apart from sanding down and painting with acrylic primer.

If you choose to decorate a previously-varnished seat, put on some rubber gloves for protection, and apply paint stripper. This will soften the varnish and you can then scrape it away with a paint scraper. You may need to apply a second coat, depending on the amount of varnish. Sand the surface to thoroughly remove traces of varnish, then coat with acrylic primer, as described below.

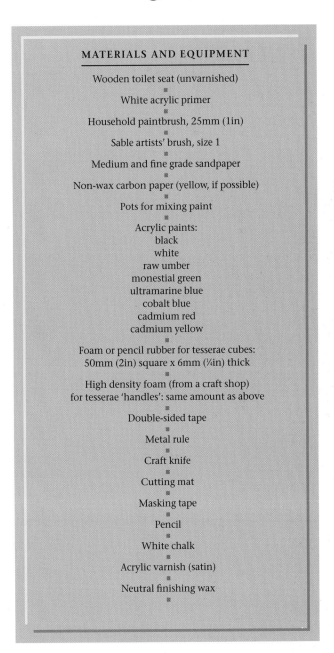

MATERIALS AND EQUIPMENT

Wooden toilet seat (unvarnished)

White acrylic primer

Household paintbrush, 25mm (1in)

Sable artists' brush, size 1

Medium and fine grade sandpaper

Non-wax carbon paper (yellow, if possible)

Pots for mixing paint

Acrylic paints:
black
white
raw umber
monestial green
ultramarine blue
cobalt blue
cadmium red
cadmium yellow

Foam or pencil rubber for tesserae cubes:
50mm (2in) square x 6mm (¼in) thick

High density foam (from a craft shop)
for tesserae 'handles': same amount as above

Double-sided tape

Metal rule

Craft knife

Cutting mat

Masking tape

Pencil

White chalk

Acrylic varnish (satin)

Neutral finishing wax

Template for Greek urn on page 128 and for shell design on page 129

1 PREPARING THE TOILET SEAT

First, remove all screws and fittings and keep them in a safe place for refitting when the project is complete. Next, sand the wooden surfaces thoroughly, first with a medium sandpaper then with a fine one.

2 Use a household brush to apply a coat of undiluted acrylic primer to all sides of the toilet seat and lid. When dry, sand down with fine grade paper to remove runs and brush marks. Repeat this process.

3 For the base coat, which represents grouting between the 'tesserae', mix half a jam-jar-full of black and white acrylic paint. Start with the white paint and gradually add the black, aiming for a medium shade of grey; dilute with water to the consistency of single cream and coat all sides of the seat and lid with this. You should find that one coat is sufficient, provided you don't thin it too much. Leave to dry.

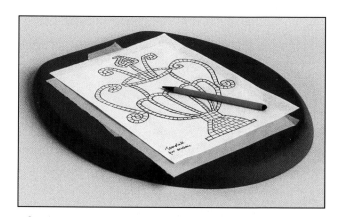

4 Trace the 'Greek urn' template on page 128, then place the tracing on the lid of the toilet seat, positioning it carefully, so that the design is straight and centred. Secure with masking tape and slide a piece of carbon paper underneath – I used a sheet of yellow carbon to show up on the grey. To transfer the design, draw over the traced shape with a pencil.

TIP
—
You may need this grey colour from time to time for any touching up, so save the surplus and replace the lid firmly on the jar.

TIP
—
If you cannot find yellow carbon paper, use yellow chalk instead. Rub the chalk onto the back of the tracing paper then, to transfer the design, position the tracing paper and retrace the design with a sharp pencil.

Close-up, showing the paint effect

Template on page 128

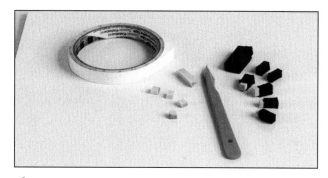

1 DECORATING THE LID

It is a good idea to make several tesserae and vary their size, as this will enable you to follow a design more easily. You can achieve a more authentic look by reprinting with another tessera the same size, but loaded with a slightly different coloured paint.

Use a craft knife and metal ruler to cut the foam into neat 6–8mm (¼–⅓in) cubes. Next, create 'handles', either by attaching 25mm (1in) pieces of high density foam to the 'tesserae' cubes with double-sided tape or, for a firmer 'handle', you can attach the cubes to the end of a pencil.

3 Touch up any overlaps, and neaten edges of the pink tesserae, by applying the grey grouting paint mix with a fine-pointed brush.

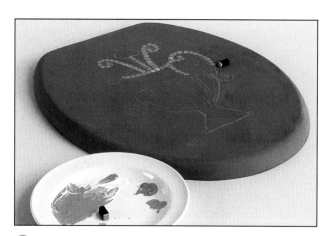

2

To print the outline, dab a cube into your paint mixture and press down onto the design – you should be able to print each one two or three times before replenishing with paint and you will find your design builds up quite quickly. Remember to vary the colour slightly, to add authenticity and realism to the 'mosaic' and to add a drop of scumble glaze to the colours in your palette to prevent them drying out too quickly.

4

Continue printing around the urn shape, with a mix of ultramarine blue, monestial green and white, following the contour, as shown. Vary the shade and intensity of the blue/green colours, by adding more white, less blue/green, or vice versa.

To reprint an area simply dab with paint and reposition on the previous mark to strengthen the shape, or to change a colour. Gradually build up the blue tesserae around the vase to the edges and along the rim of the lid.

> ## TIP
>
> *Paint a piece of card with the grey base coat and experiment with printing your tesserae – notice how different colours look on the grey background. I chose shades of pink for the outline of the Greek urn, mixed from red, yellow and white acrylic paints, with contrasting shades of blue and green printed around the motif.*

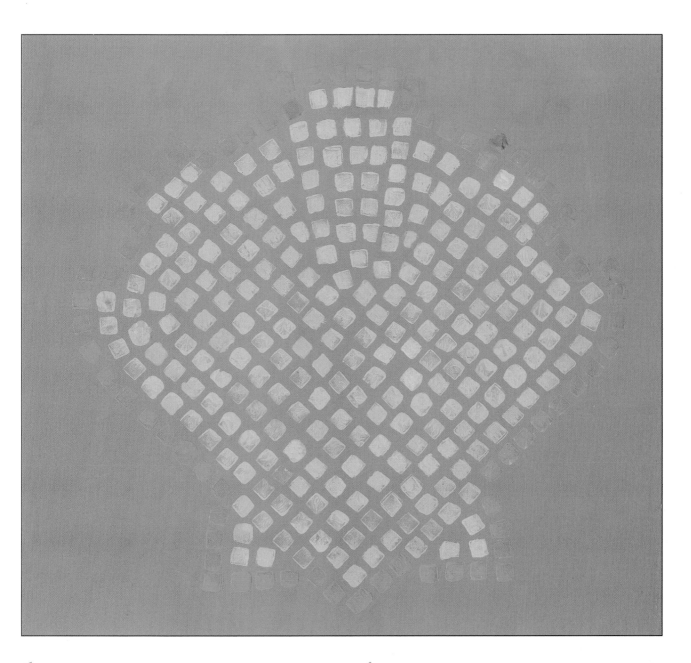

1 **DECORATING THE UNDERSIDE OF THE LID**
Apply grey base coat and leave to dry.

2 Photocopy the shell template on page 129 (onto tracing paper if possible), position it centrally on the underside of the seat. Secure it with masking tape, slide carbon paper underneath, then trace, pressing firmly with a sharp pencil. Remove the tracing paper.

3 Start with the shaded tesserae, on the edge of the design, to emphasize the outline shape. For this, I mixed a bright salmon colour with 1 teaspoon of white paint, a quarter teaspoon each of cadmium red and yellow ochre and 1 teaspoon of scumble glaze. Dip your tesserae into this, each time printing two or three times, until the shape is complete.

4 Mix some paler pink by adding a half teaspoon of white and a half teaspoon of scumble glaze to the above mix and use this to fill in the remaining shell shape. If any have not printed very well, simply reposition the tessera and print over the same area. Use the grey base coat with a size 1 sable brush if you need to neaten up.

5 To complete the design, mix a quarter teaspoon of monestial green with 1 teaspoon white acrylic and a half teaspoon of scumble glaze. Use this mixture to cover the remaining area on the underside of the lid. Follow the outline of the shell and print right around each time, so that the design builds up in 'bands'. After three or four bands around the shell, fill in the remaining area more randomly.

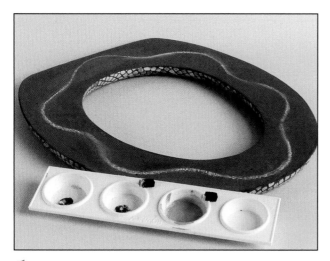

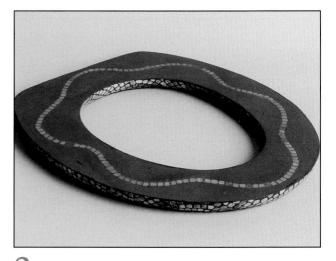

1 DECORATING THE SEAT

Draw a simple design with white chalk on the underside of the seat, using the illustration as a guide.

As seat shapes vary, it is best to draw one side, then repeat the same design on the opposite side. The chalk will wipe off easily with a damp cloth, once your single row of mosaic has been applied.

2
Follow the the chalk outline with a single row of printed tesserae.

3
Add more 'tesserae' around the inside edge – I have used a darker shade of green to create contrast.

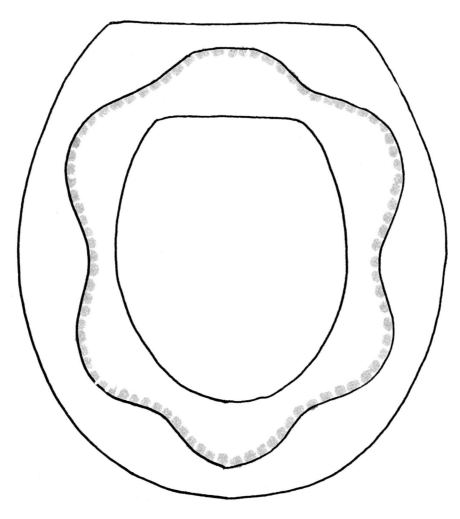

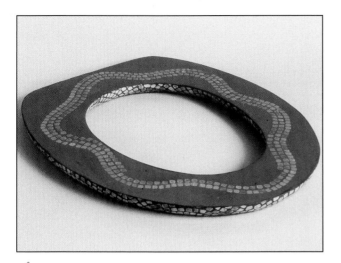

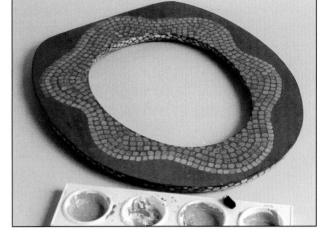

4 Continue until the underside of the seat is covered.

5 Repeat the design on the top of the seat and infill with printed tesserae until the whole seat is covered, top and bottom.

6 When the paint is dry, apply two coats of satin varnish to all sides of the seat and lid and leave until thoroughly dry.

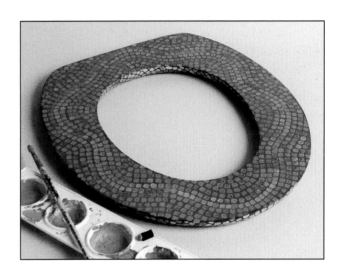

7 As a final protection to the faux mosaic, apply a 'neutral' finishing wax with a brush or cloth. Wait for ten minutes or so, then buff to a soft hard sheen with a cloth. Your seat is now complete, and the fixings can be replaced.

CELEBRATION TRAY
using the grisaille technique

I was recently asked for a commemorative painting as a gift to mark a fiftieth wedding anniversary. The gift was in the form of a trompe l'oeil painted tray, depicting the wedding photograph of 1948, a lace-edged tray cloth, an envelope with the names of the couple and a photograph of their two daughters as children. I rummaged in a shop dealing in old stamps and came across a 1948 stamp, showing the heads of King George and Queen Elizabeth in the commemorative year of their Silver Wedding anniversary. I duly copied this onto the envelope bearing the address of the church where the wedding took place. The extra painted details tell us more about the people involved and the times they lived in, as well as being especially significant to them by telling their story in a visual way. I also painted confetti scattered across the surface – as well as adding colour and depth to the composition, it was a decorative way of signifying a wedding celebration. The lace cloth and embroidered details add to the sense of occasion. The border has been decorated with gold leaf to signify a Golden Wedding anniversary and, to give the photographs a period feel, I painted them using the grisaille technique.

The celebration tray project that follows is a simplified version of my commissioned tray, without the envelope and the children's photograph. But of course, you can adapt the idea as you wish, and add memorabilia of your own choosing.

MATERIALS AND EQUIPMENT

Wooden tray, approx. 45 x 30cm (18 x 12in)

Photograph of your choice

White acrylic primer

Household brush, 25mm (1in)

Flat, nylon, artists' brush: 12mm (½in)

Sable artists' brush, size 1

Fine grade sandpaper

Acrylic paints:
monestial green
ultramarine
raw umber
cadmium red
cadmium yellow

See-through masking tape (Scotch Magic™ Tape)

Non-wax carbon paper

Pencil

Plastic ruler – short length (30cm/1ft)

Set square

Dutch gold metal leaf (one and a half sheets needed)

Water-based gold leaf medium

Medium scissors

Soft cotton cloth

Acrylic varnish (satin)

Detail of the commissioned wedding anniversary tray

 Template for lace cloth on page 130

43

1 PREPARING THE TRAY

Use the household brush to prime the surface and sides of the tray with white acrylic primer. Once dry, sand down with fine grade sandpaper and apply another coat. Sand again once dry.

2

For the soft shade of eau de nil (shown top right), mix a quantity of white, and add monestial green, a little ultramarine blue, and a very small amount of raw umber to mellow the shade slightly. Add a little water to aid mixing. Aim for half a jam-jar-full, which should be adequate for two coats of paint, as well as touching up between stages and the shadow base needed for stage 3 on page 48. You need only sand if the brush marks are too obvious.

4

Use a pencil and ruler to mark a 12mm (½in) wide border, approximately 40mm (1½in) from the edges of the tray. Don't worry, at this stage, about it overlapping the outline of the cloth.

5

Stick Scotch Magic™ Tape around all sides of the border to define the edges before painting. Then mix some red and burnt umber acrylic (as a base coat for the

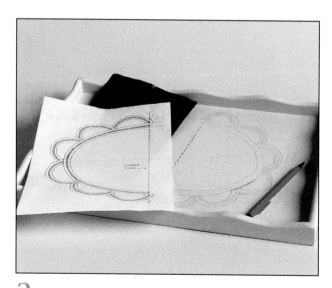

3

If necessary, enlarge the 'lace cloth' template on page 130 to size on a photocopier and trace over it. Position the tracing on the tray – slightly off centre to add interest – and pencil over the design. Turn the template and trace the other half of the cloth onto the tray to complete the oval.

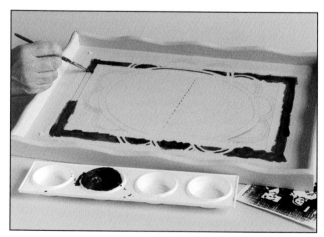

Here, the edges are masked with ordinary masking tape, but use Scotch Magic ™ Tape if you are a beginner

gold leaf), and thin with just a little water – if you use too much it may run under the masking tape; for the same reason, apply the paint away from the tape, not towards it. Be careful you don't paint over the 'lace' edges of the cloth, as the border should show through. Once the paint is dry, remove the tape to reveal the border. If you find any touching up is necessary, use a fine brush and the eau de nil paint you have saved in a jam jar.

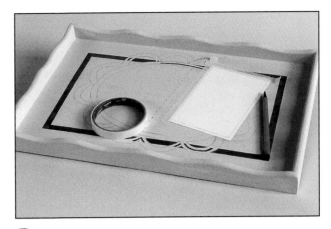

1 POSITIONING THE PHOTOGRAPH

First, photocopy your photograph in black and white, reducing or enlarging it as necessary. Trim the image to size (mine was 15 x 10cm/6 x 4in), using a ruler and set square to check right angles. Position the photocopy on the tray and pencil round the shape.

2
Remove the photocopy and fix masking tape around the edge of the rectangle, to mask off the area for painting. Apply an even coat of white acrylic primer with the flat artists' brush, remembering, as before, to paint away from the taped edge. Once the paint is dry, remove the tape to reveal a neat area of white paint. Measure in 6mm (¼in) from the edge all round, to create a border.

3
Again apply masking tape, this time to butt up with the inner outline (i.e. the edge of the 'photograph') and protect the border. Mix a quarter teaspoon of raw umber with a teaspoon of white to make a medium tone and apply this to the masked area with a flat artists' brush. Once the paint is dry, remove the tape.

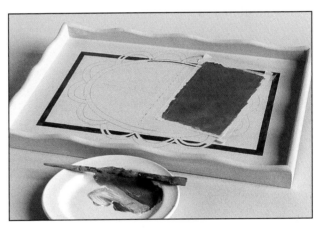

4
Trace the main details from the photocopy of your photograph, position the tracing in the painted rectangle, and fix with a couple of strips of masking tape. Slide the carbon paper underneath and transfer the details.

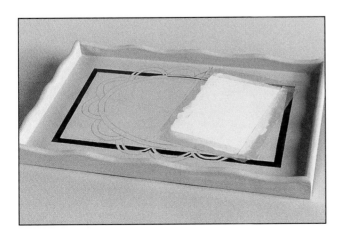

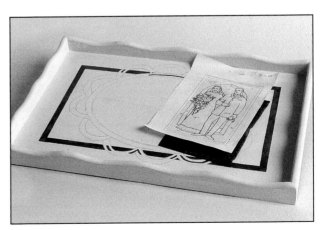

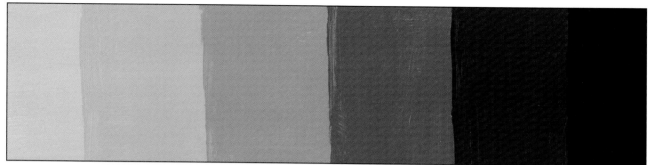

Illustration showing shades of raw umber, ranging from light to dark with the addition of white and black paint

Photograph and outline drawing, showing light (L), medium (M) and dark (D) areas

THE GRISAILLE TECHNIQUE

Use shades of one colour to re-create the photograph. You will find that a very wide range of tones can be achieved with the addition of black and white. I chose raw umber, a cool brown colour, to give a faded 'sepia' effect and mixed a little scumble glaze with the different shades at each stage, to make it easier to blend the tones and to keep the paint workable for longer. (See also pages 16–17.)

1 Mix a range of tones on your palette from raw umber, white, and black acrylic. Start with white, thinned with a little water, then add a small amount of raw umber. When mixed, paint a sample of this onto a piece of card. Add a little more raw umber to the same mixture, and paint this next to the first sample. A progression of shades will gradually develop, until you reach the darkest shade, the pure raw umber colour. To darken this, you need only add a little black paint.

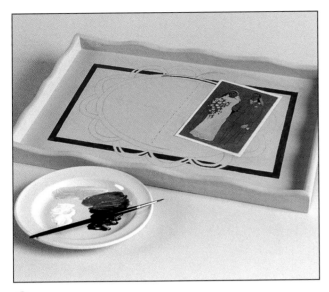

1 PAINTING THE LACE CLOTH

Mask off the photo edge, to protect it. Mix a pale cream colour with white and a very little yellow ochre, and paint in the oval shape of the cloth with a flat artists' brush. If necessary, apply a second coat. Next, paint in the scalloped edges with a fine artists' brush.

2 With your outlines in place, refer to the photograph on the previous page for light, medium and dark areas, and to the colour swatch for the range of colours. First, mix an off-white shade with a little raw umber and white and use this to paint the lightest areas, starting with the dress – the largest and lightest area; next paint the flowers, veil, shirt, buttonhole, gloves etc, for which I added more white and a small amount of raw umber.

2 To indicate folds, pencil faint lines across the width and length of the cloth. Darken the mixture of yellow ochre and white paint with some raw umber and add

3 Add the dark areas – the hair and areas behind the dress, between the flowers, and the eyes – using raw umber either neat or with a little white.

4 To add detail to the bouquet, paint a small dark dot in the centre of each flower. Next, paint the shadows beneath the figures quite loosely – so that the background colour shows through – using raw umber diluted with water to make a thin translucent wash. Leave to dry.

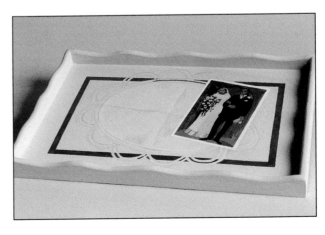

water to dilute to a milky consistency. Apply this as a wash, to create shadows on the left side and below the pencilled fold lines. To complete the illusion of folds, paint highlights next to and above any 'shadowed' areas, using a fine brush and diluted white paint. Once the paint is dry, remove the masking tape to reveal the neat edge of the photograph.

TIP
—
Rolling the brush tip against the palette takes off any excess paint and ensures a good 'point' when painting fine detail.

4 Paint tiny lines of stitching between the double lines of the scalloped edging, using the cream paint mixed for stage 1, 'Painting the lace cloth' (see page 47), and a size 1 paintbrush. Then use the 'shadow' mix to paint shadows for the lace threads across each scallop. The highlights will be added later.

USING GOLD LEAF

Next, apply gold leaf around the edge of the tray border. I used one and a half sheets of Dutch metal leaf, which is sold in loose sheets of around 20 to a pack. Fold a sheet with its tissue backing paper, and use scissors to cut into strips slightly wider than the 12mm (½in) border. Cut more strips as necessary.

3 To create the shadows around the tray cloth and photograph, add some monestial green and a little raw umber to your ready-mixed background colour (stage 2, page 44), to produce a darker, more vivid shade. Dilute the mixture with water – to achieve two teaspoons of thinned paint – and add some scumble glaze; use a size 1 brush to paint in the shadows with this mix. In this case, the light direction comes from the top left, casting shadows on the right and bottom edges of the photo, so paint between the double lines of the cloth edge and the scalloped edge to ensure stitching lines show up.

1 Carefully brush on the gold leaf medium which makes the gold leaf adhere – keeping it within the border. When the medium is dry, it will become quite glossy, and very tacky to the touch, so you can see if you have covered the area evenly.

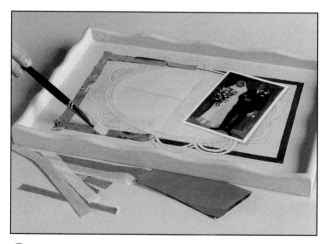

2 After the prescribed drying time, remove the tissue paper from the gold strips, carefully place them over the border and press down first with a dry paintbrush, then with a clean dry cloth to position it firmly. Don't worry if the delicate gold breaks as you position it, the pieces will stick all the same. The gold leaf may look untidy at this stage, but it will only adhere to the areas painted with the medium. Once it is firmly in place, brush away any excess to reveal the neat gold border. If some small areas have been missed this won't matter, as the red colour of the border will show through, as intended, to give an 'antique' look. However, if you want to fill in the gaps, re-apply the medium to the areas you have missed, and follow the same procedure. If there are any metallic marks around the gold, a damp cloth should remove them.

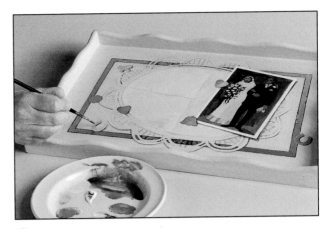

1 ADDING THE DETAILS

Trace the confetti shown below, then transfer the tracing to the tray using carbon paper. Position it in a scattered arrangement – placing it against the 'photograph' will strengthen the illusion.

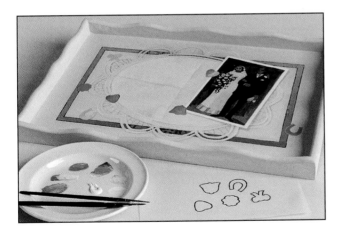

2 Paint in the confetti, using a fine brush and a variety of pale shades of blue, pink, yellow and green. It won't matter if you paint over the gold areas, as long as the paint is not diluted too much.

3 Using the same 'shadow' colour as for stage 3 on page 48, paint shadows to the left and bottom of the confetti shapes. Follow the direction of the shadows around the photograph and, where the confetti overlaps the 'photograph', overpaint with the 'shadow' mix.

4 With white paint, and a fine brush, paint the connecting lines of lace in the scalloped edges, following the darker shadowed lines painted previously.

Finally, although this is a decorative item, it would be lovely to use as it is intended on special occasions and this would be a very subtle way to show off your handiwork. To protect the surface I would suggest using three coats of satin varnish, sanding with fine grade paper between coats when dry. The surface will then resist heat and stains and will need only an occasional wipe with a damp cloth.

4 OCCASIONAL TABLE

with a collection of shells and a small lace cloth arranged on some terracotta tiles

The table I used for this project is approximately 30 x 40cm (12 x 16in) and stands 51cm (20in) high. The top, which has a routed edge, is made from MDF and the legs are made from beech wood. You should be able to purchase a similar-size table, ready for painting, from a DIY shop. Alternatively you could apply this design to a table of a different size and adjust the template accordingly.

Paint can easily be made to imitate the warm, rustic texture and colour of terracotta, which will add a Mediterranean look to a surface. Here, I have created the handmade look of terracotta tiles on a table, but the technique described could equally well be used on a wall. A collection of shells and a lace cloth painted in trompe l'oeil style complete the illusion.

MATERIALS AND EQUIPMENT

Small table (see above)
∎
Fine grade sandpaper and sanding block
∎
White acrylic primer
∎
Acrylic paints:
yellow ochre
raw sienna
white
burnt umber
black
cobalt blue
purple
cadmium red
cadmium yellow
raw umber
∎
Small natural sponges
∎
Fine and medium brushes: artists' sable, size 1
∎
Scumble glaze
∎
Acrylic varnish (dead flat)
∎
Ruler
∎
T-square
∎
Pencil
∎
A narrow length of wooden moulding (see page 53, stage 2)
∎
Tracing paper
∎
Non-wax carbon paper
∎

1 PREPARING THE SURFACE

First sand all surfaces, paying special attention to the corners of the table top and the legs. A rigid sanding block is useful for these edges.

2

Apply two coats of acrylic primer to the entire table, turning the table around as you paint – make sure you don't miss any areas, especially around the legs. Sand between coats, once the paint is dry, to remove drips around legs and brush marks on the table surface.

 Template for lace cloth and shells on page 131

Template for lace cloth and shells on page 131

51

3 Mix some yellow ochre with a little raw sienna and thin with water to the consistency of single cream. Sponge this mix onto the surface and edges of the table top, aiming for a lightly textured effect, with the white paint still showing through in some areas. Once the top is evenly covered, leave it to dry for 20 minutes or so.

4 Next, add some raw sienna and scumble glaze to the same mix, to make a deeper shade of yellow ochre. Apply this lightly and evenly with a clean sponge, again allowing some of the paler colour to show through the open texture and aiming, with each successive layer of colour, to add further depth and character.

5 Now use a clean sponge to apply white paint, thinned to thin cream consistency. This will give a chalky effect, yet still have the appearance of a bright-coloured terracotta.

If, like me, you prefer a pale terracotta, apply another sponging of white paint once the first coat has dried.

6 Protect the table top with one coat of dead flat varnish, before going on to the next stage.

Sponging on white paint (see stage 5)

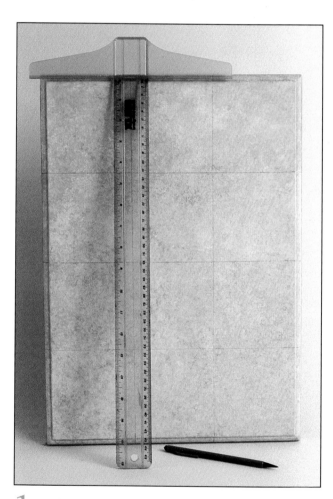

1 **ADDING THE TILES AND LACE CLOTH**
Once the varnish is dry, divide the table top into individual tiles, using a pencil and ruler to mark out the chosen number. I have used a 10cm (4in) unit of measurement, which gives me four tiles across the top and three tiles down either side. It is important to check the accuracy of the straight lines with a set square at this stage, as precise measurements are crucial.

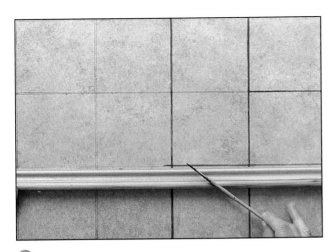

2 The next stage is to paint in the grouting, to complete the illusion of tiles. For this, mix a medium grey acrylic, and add some burnt umber for warmth. Rest the metal part of the loaded brush on a piece of wooden moulding, to guide your hand, and pull downwards from the top, using even pressure, to paint a straight line. Repeat along all the pencilled lines.

TIP

Practice is all that is necessary to perfect this time-saving technique of painting lines, so experiment on a piece of scrap before attempting the 'grouting' on the actual project.

3 Copy the template of the lace cloth and shells design (see page 131) and trace it onto the table top (see instructions on page 124). Paint in the lace cloth first – aiming to create a subtle shade, using white with a touch of cobalt blue and black.

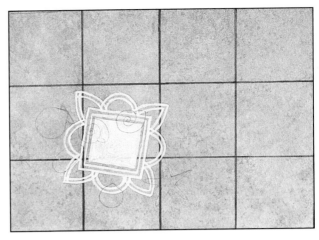

4 Don't worry if you paint over the pencilled shell outline, simply wait until the paint is dry, reposition the template and draw the shells in again, with clear outlines.

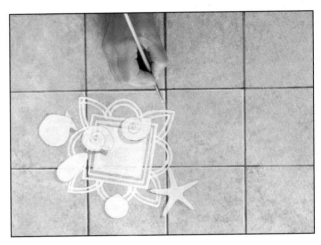

1 **PAINTING THE SHELLS**

To make the shells three-dimensional, paint in the shadows to one side of each one (in this case the shadow is falling to the right-hand side) using a mixture of grey, cobalt blue and a touch of purple. Build up the shadow gradually, by applying the paint in thin transparent layers. Next, paint a narrow white line with a fine brush, to the right and below to highlight the 'grouted' edges.

2 Now paint in the shells – each one a slightly different colour – using subtle pinks, yellow ochre and warm browns. Aim at first for flat colours then, once the first layer is dry, paint in a darker shade, generally keeping to one side of each shell, to create a curved effect. Paint in the shadow of the lace cloth, using grey with cobalt blue and a touch of purple.

3 Paint the details and markings on each shell, referring to the life-size artwork above. Once the details are dry, paint in the highlights: use a diluted white, so the layers are transparent and the details are not obscured. When this is dry, paint in the small, sharper highlights using undiluted white acrylic.

1 THE FINISHING TOUCHES

Now paint in the edges of the lace cloth, the tiny straight lines of stitching, and the larger lacy threads inside the scalloped edges. A size 1 sable brush is best for this, because it is very fine and has a good point.

3 Add further character to the tiles, with a few 'cracks'. First lightly pencil in the cracks, then paint the darker lines, with a dark terracotta shade mixed from grey and burnt umber. When dry, paint a white line, following the shape of the darker lines, to give the illusion of fine cracks on the surface.

The table is now complete and ready for use but, if you would like a practical, wipe-down surface, varnish first with two coats of 'dead flat' varnish.

2 Mask out three tiles to create some authentic variation – sponging over some white paint on one tile, stippling a darker terracotta shade on another, and a pale terracotta on the third. Aim for subtlety of contrast but also to give the tiles an individual, handmade look. Once the paint is dry, remove the masking tape.

FAUX MARBLE TABLE TOP

with folded check cloth

MATERIALS AND EQUIPMENT

Unvarnished wooden table
(top approx. 30 x 45cm/12 x 18in)

Fine grade sandpaper and sanding block

White acrylic primer

1 litre cream vinyl matt emulsion paint

Acrylic paints:
cobalt blue;
purple;
raw umber;
cadmium yellow;
yellow ochre;
cadmium red;
monestial green;
white;
black;
ultramarine

Scumble glaze

Small palette with cups

Badger softening brush

Round stippling brush

Small natural sponge

Acrylic varnish ('dead flat')

Non-wax carbon paper

Tracing paper

Bottle top (see page 61, stage 1)

Transparent masking tape (Scotch Magic™ Tape)

Pencil

Sable artists' brush, size 1 or 2

Chisel-edge paintbrush, 30mm (1¼in)

Flat paintbrush, 12mm (½in)

Light-coloured Letraset (see page 63, stage 3)

This project includes basic marbling techniques, as well as a template for a check cloth with realistic folds and advice on how to achieve convincing painted shadows. The illusion is enhanced by the inclusion of a tempting packet of painted sweets. If you do not have a suitable unvarnished table, buy one from a DIY shop.

1 Sand all surfaces, using the sanding block, paying special attention to the corners of the table top and the legs. Apply acrylic primer all over, allow to dry, then sand. Apply another coat and repeat the process.

2 Next, apply a base coat of cream emulsion, to form a smooth and even surface for the marbling. This can be a ready-mixed colour from a DIY store, or you can mix your own neutral brown shade by adding raw umber to white paint. If you wish, add a touch of yellow ochre for a slightly richer tint. When dry, sand down for an even finish. Finally, prior to marbling, apply one even coat of dead flat varnish, which will dry very quickly.

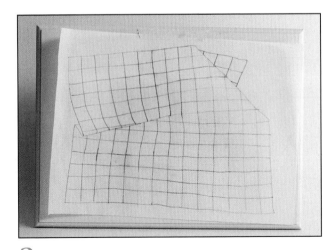

3 Photocopy the two cloth templates (see pages 132–3) onto tracing paper and join up the centre line with 'Scotch Magic ™ Tape' to make a complete template. As this is almost transparent, you can position the tracing on

 Template for cloth on pages 132–3 and for sweet packet on page 134

the table, secure it with tape and slide some carbon paper underneath. Only trace the outline of the cloth at this stage, pressing firmly with the pencil for a crisp image. This will determine the area to be marbled and the area to be painted as folded cloth. Remove the tracing paper to reveal the outline of the cloth.

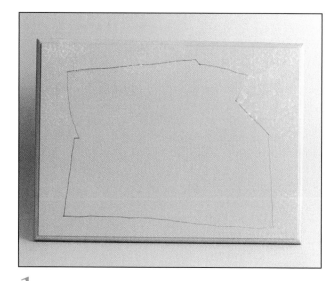

1 THE MARBLE BASE

For the marble base colour, mix a white glaze, with a half teaspoon each of white paint and scumble glaze, thinned with water, and a brown glaze with the same amount of raw umber, scumble glaze and water. Apply the white glaze first, to the surface around the traced outline, using a stippling brush or sponge. Aim for a 'broken' effect – allowing some of the base coat to show through – and leave some areas clear to apply a brown glaze. Next, apply the brown glaze in areas adjacent to the white, and merge the edges of the brown and white glazes. While the paint is still damp, lightly brush the surface with a badger brush, to soften and blend the two shades.

2

Dip a fine brush into the brown glaze and, holding the brush loosely, roll it between finger and thumb, and apply the paint across and downwards in a continuous line, so that the thickness of the line varies. The veining must be kept more or less in one direction – running diagonally from one side to the other. If you want a darker colour, just add a touch more raw umber. While the paint is still damp, brush in several directions over the surface with a badger brush, to soften the painted areas and create layers.

TIP

For a subtler look to the veining, rub the surface with fine grade finishing paper. This will 'cut back' the surface and soften the contrast.

3 Continue to build up a network of lines in this way, adding more veining with the white glaze and crossing over some of the softened darker veins. If your table top has a shaped or flat edge, remember to continue the glazes and veining on these surfaces too. If you feel there might be too many veins, or you want to add more glaze to some areas, simply stipple over with either white or brown glaze.

1 **THE CLOTH BACKGROUND**
Next, mix a subtle off-white shade for the folded cloth, from white with a touch each of cobalt blue and black and use a flat brush to paint up to the pencilled outline. The final white highlights, painted at a later stage, will be much more effective against this off-white colour.

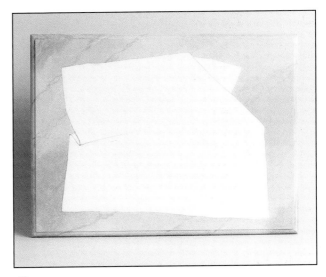

4 While the paint is still damp, use the badger brush to give a final softening to the surface and, when the marbling is dry, brush with fast-drying 'dead flat' varnish slightly over the pencilled edge.

2 Using the same traced template for the cloth, match the outline and carefully draw in the fold lines at the centre and top right with carbon paper. These lines describe the shape of the ripples and folds and the position of the painted shadows.

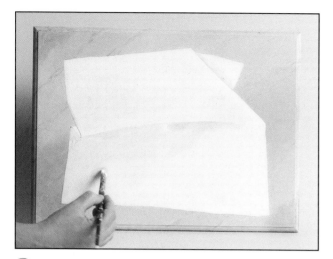

3 To add interest to the surface of the cloth, vary the colour to suggest ripples and undulations. Using the same off-white cloth colour, add a touch more blue and black and a very small touch of purple to deepen the tone slightly. Aim for a subtle colour change, with the darkest areas of paint in the fold at the centre. Use almost dry colour on your brush to merge the darker colour into the painted white cloth.

Intensify the darker tones of the shadows by slightly deepening the colours.

2 For the two-tone gingham check shown, mix cobalt blue and white to make the dark blue and, using a size 1 or 2 sable brush with a good point, carefully paint the outline of each square.

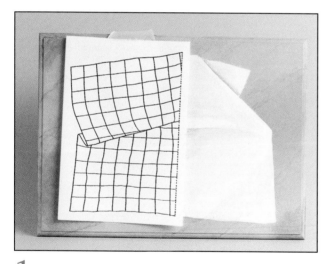

1 **ADDING THE CHECKS**
Carefully re-position the tracing over the outline and, using the same procedure as before, trace the lines across and down to create the checks. You may need to strengthen the design with darker pencil lines, but now the basic check outlines are clear and ready to paint.

3 Fill in the outlines with a chisel-edged brush, starting with two complete rows at the top and at the right hand side, as this will make the pattern easier to follow.

4 The pale blue squares can now be painted between the darker ones. Mix more of the same colour but add a lot more white. Follow the procedure as before, until the pale blue squares are complete.

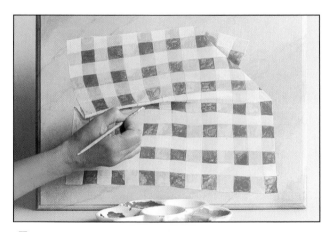

5 To accentuate the central and top right folds, darken each square underneath the fold with a mix of cobalt blue and a touch of purple. A very thinned mix of cobalt, tinted with black and purple washed across this area will blend the darker squares without leaving a line. The top right hand corner fold can be tinted in the same way.

6 Next, add the shadow of the cloth on the marbled surface. Following the outline of the cloth, pencil a guide line about 6mm (¼in) out from the hem along the left hand side, and bottom.

Make sure the surface is flat, to avoid the paint running, then use a fine brush and some very dilute raw umber and cobalt paint in the shadow between the cloth and your guide line. Allow the paint to dry, then apply more of the same paint, adjusting the intensity of colour with successive tints. As the marble has had a previous layer of flat varnish, using a damp cloth will wipe away any hard lines that might occur.

1 **THE SWEET PACKET**

To complete the illusion I have added an open packet of sweets, to tempt the onlooker. Trace the template on page 134, secure the tracing in position with masking tape, then pencil in the outline of the sweet packet and the circles for the sweets. Block in with cadmium yellow, mixed with a little white paint to make it cover better.

Use a bottle top to print the round sweets. First, mix a bright colour such as orange, paint the printing area of the bottle top with a loaded paintbrush, press it firmly down to create a perfect circle, then fill in with the remaining colour. Use the same method for each coloured sweet, cleaning the bottle top between colours.

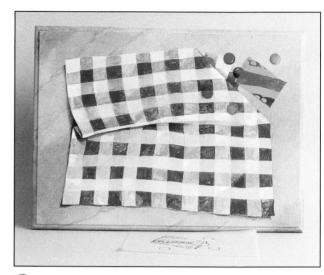

2 When the yellow sweet packet is dry, reposition the tracing paper template and draw the remaining design onto the yellow paint. Next, paint in the design with 'flat' colour.

 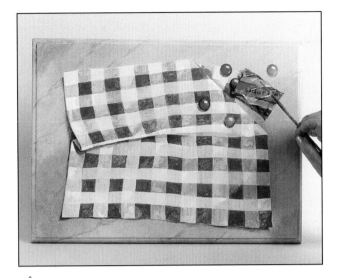

3 Slightly darken the yellow ochre paint with cobalt blue, and blend this colour into the yellow to add form and shape along the bottom edge (see colour drawing on facing page) and to wash over any hard edges to give a crumpled effect to the sweet wrapper. Next, wash over the central diagonal band with a very thinned and darkened red paint. This rough wash will make the packet look crinkly, because the yellow will show through. Make sure you work on a flat surface, so the paint doesn't run.

For the lettering on the sweet packet, use Letraset, which is quick and simple to use and readily available from stationers. Choose a brightly coloured type and press the letters firmly in place, to follow the slightly crumpled surface, then 'flat' paint a thinned darker red wash over the letters.

4 Next, paint flashes of white lines on the surface with a fine brush, to create the hard glossy highlights. You can also use thinned white paint as a wash, to create a glossed-over effect on top of the 'flashes'.

Use raw umber and cobalt as before, for the darkened edge of the shadow over the marbled surface and cloth. Pencil in the shadows of the sweets on the cloth first, following the circular shape; use dark blue with purple wash and build up intensity with successive applications. Adding small painted white dots on each sweet will create mouthwatering highlights.

Finally, to protect the surface of the table, apply two coats of dead flat acrylic varnish and your table top is complete.

TROMPE L'OEIL
STONE WINDOW

For this project an unvarnished wooden panel – the type made for kitchen unit cupboards – provides the ideal surface to paint on. I have chosen to use the reverse of the panel, as it is a much simpler shape and suits the design of the trompe l'oeil window. A faux 'stone' effect has been applied to the frame with shadows and highlights, to create a rounded carved edge. In the foreground, framing the coloured glass window surround, painted leaves and flowers soften the straight lines of the window and add colour and contrast to the foreground. The view through the window suggests a summer's day, and I have kept the colours fairly pale and low contrast by mixing them with white, to create an impression of distance.

When finished, the panel becomes a truly portable trompe l'oeil window, ready to create visual trickery and maximum impact on a plain windowless wall. It would look perfect in a corner without natural light, where subtle lighting would gently illuminate the painting.

MATERIALS AND EQUIPMENT

Unvarnished wooden panel,
approx. 90cm (3ft) tall by 30cm (12in)

Non-clogging finishing paper

White acrylic primer

Ruler

Pencil

T-square

Masking tape

Acrylic paints:
yellow ochre; raw umber; white; cobalt blue;
ultramarine blue; purple; monestial green; violet; black;
cadmium yellow

Scumble glaze

Badger softening brush

Flat paintbrushes: 12mm (½in) and 25mm (1in)·

Stippling brushes: 25mm (1in) round
and oblong 100 x 25mm (4 x 1in)

Artists' paintbrushes: sable size 1, flat size 4

Tracing paper

Sponge

Transparent masking tape (Scotch Magic™ Tape)

Straightedge

Carbon paper

Stencil card (see pages 124–5)

Stencil brush

Cutting knife

Clean cotton cloth

Acrylic varnish ('dead flat')

Detail of the butterfly on corner of the carved stonework

 Templates for flowers, leaves and window on pages 134 and 135.

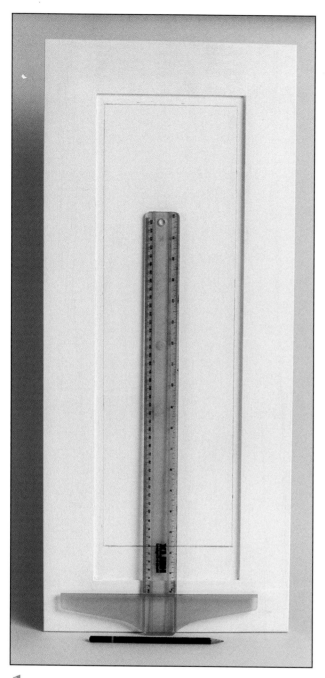

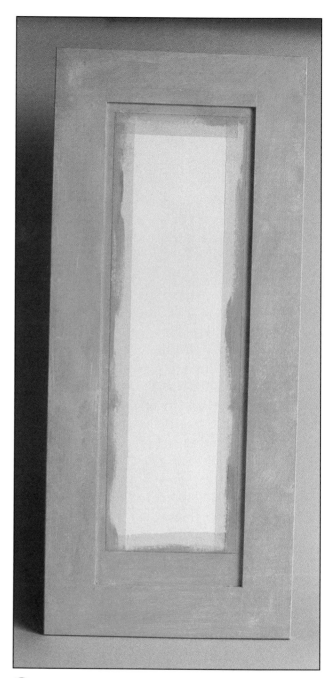

1 THE WINDOW FRAME

Sand down the panel, then coat with acrylic primer. Allow the paint to dry, sand, and apply another coat. Once dry, sand again. Draw a line within the centre panel with a pencil and ruler, 1cm (⅜in) from the top and sides but 5cm (2in) from the bottom of the panel, to give extra thickness and solidity to the 'stone' sill.

2 Lay strips of masking tape around the inside edges of the pencil line, to protect the inner panel, then paint the frame with a tablespoon of yellow ochre and half a teaspoon of white acrylic, thinned with water to thin cream consistency. You should find that one coat is sufficient.

3 Mix some raw umber with a touch of yellow ochre and a dollop of scumble glaze, and thin with water to the consistency of single cream. Stipple this mixture onto the base coat, until evenly covered. The stippling will leave areas of base coat showing and create the texture of crumbly stone. Once the paint is dry, apply a coat of 'dead flat' varnish to smooth and seal the surface, and make further paint easier to apply.

4 Rule diagonal lines from the four corners of the frame to represent mitre joints, then measure 1cm (⅜in) in from the outside edge of the frame, and pencil in a rectangle, inside the frame.

5 Next, you need to transform the flat stone window frame into a thicker, rounded stone frame. To do this, take each section at a time, starting with the vertical left hand section, and protecting the adjoining sections with strips of masking tape. The light on the frame is coming from the left and above, so my highlight is on the left.

For this, dilute some white paint with water and, using a 12mm (½in) brush, and a straightedge to ensure a regular line, paint a line along one side of the centre section. Now paint another line – this time with more water than paint – to overlap the first and soften the edge. Leave to dry.

6 Continue with the other sections – protecting the adjoining sections with masking tape, as before – and applying highlights to the left hand and uppermost areas of stone moulding in each section.

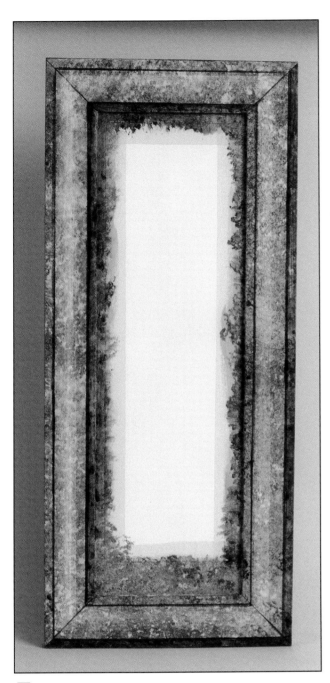
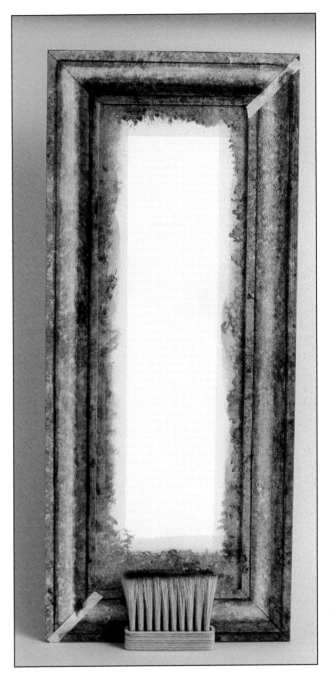

7 To strengthen the pencilled lines, paint over them with slightly diluted raw umber using a fine artists' brush with a good point. Don't forget that the shadow will fall on the underside (i.e. bottom) of each horizontal section.

8 To make the 'roundness' of the frame more convincing, blend darker colour on the right-hand areas of moulding. Dilute some raw umber with water and a little scumble glaze and paint an even line, about 2.5cm (1in) wide, along the vertical section. Immediately press the oblong stippler into the wet paint and blend towards the centre to softly merge the colour. Continue with all four sections then, once the paint is dry, remove the masking tape.

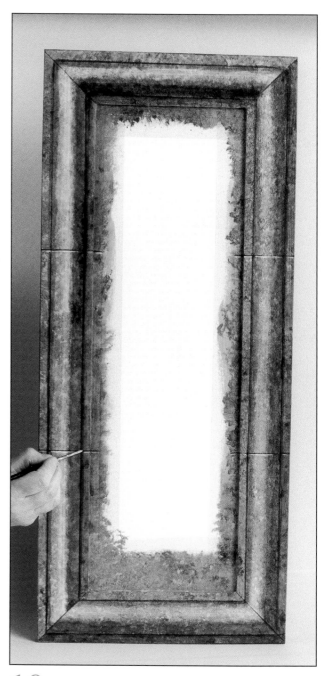

9 Next, divide the frame into smaller, brick-like sections, by dividing the overall height by three (i.e. into 30cm/12in sections), using a T-square and pencil. Mix some raw umber with a little black and, with a fine brush, paint a thin horizontal line across the two sides of the frame, just above the pencil lines. With the same brush and colour pick out a few small 'holes', in the form of dots, to create texture here and there in the stone.

10 Now load a brush with white paint, thinned with a little water, and paint lines the same width as, and immediately below, the darker lines. With the same brush and colour, add a few highlights to the bottom edge of the 'dots' applied as texture in the previous stage.

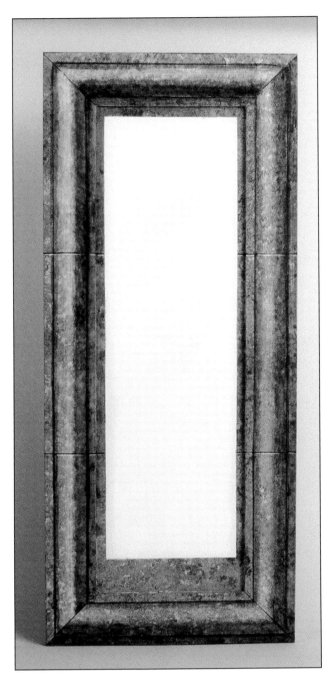

11 Once satisfied with the overall effect, remove the tape and leave the frame to dry for at least four hours.

1 **THE VIEW THROUGH THE WINDOW**
Protect the completed frame with masking tape while painting the view, lining up the tape with the inside edge of the 'stone' frame. Paint the sky first, mixing cobalt blue and white with a little scumble glaze and diluting with water. Start at the top of the picture, applying the paint with a flat 25mm (1in) brush and work across the painting, away from the masking tape and towards the middle. Gradually add more white as you work downwards, overlapping the previous paint each time. Work very quickly and use a badger softening brush across the damp paint to remove brush marks and to blend the shades together. The horizon – roughly half way down the picture – should be almost white.

> **TIP**
>
> *If you add a very small amount of yellow ochre to the white, it will add a lovely subtle tint to an otherwise flat white area of sky. Use the badger softener again, to blend the colours, then leave to dry.*

2 Mix some ultramarine blue with a small amount of purple and white – aim for a pale colour, to indicate that the mountains are a long way away. Use this mixture to roughly block in the mountains with a flat brush.

3 Add a little more blue to the mixture and, as you move down, paint a lower range of hills, making the colours slightly more intense as you work towards the foreground.

4 Add a touch of green to the blue and apply this as a flat horizontal strip below the blue hills, adding a few dots here and there to read as distant clumps of trees. Add yellow to create another horizontal strip in the middle distance, and finally shades of green, becoming darker in the immediate foreground with the addition of raw umber.

5 Stencilling is the quickest way to apply the repeated shapes of the overhanging leaves and flowers in the foreground. First, cut several-sized shapes for the leaves at the top left of the frame, using the template on page 134. Then mix some raw umber and monestial green for the darkest leaves – position the stencil randomly and apply the paint with a stencil brush. Mix a brighter green for the next layer, then mix green with yellow and a little white for the foreground leaves. Repeat several times, sometimes overlapping the leaves for a natural look. To eliminate that hard-edged 'printed' effect, use a fine artists' brush – while the paint is still wet – to neaten the edges and to elongate the tips of the leaves.

6 Add lighter green to the final layer of leaves in the top left, painting the stems and tapering the tips of the leaves. Then cut another stencil for the more rounded leaves in the lower foreground (see template on page 134). Mix some monestial green with black, and paint in some leaves with this darker mixture, using the colour neat to prevent the paint 'bleeding' under the stencil. Next, mix some purple with a touch of black and print some stencilled flowers (see template on page 134) – printing one flower over another to create a cluster of flowers.

7 Mix a light purple, with purple and white. Reposition the stencil over each flower in turn and dab the colour around the tips of the petals. Finally, use a fine brush to give each flower a yellow ochre centre.

8 With the view complete and dry, measure approximately 6mm (¼in) from the taped edge and draw a line all around the inside. With a steady hand paint between the tape and the pencil line using a dark grey paint, to form a 'leaded' frame between the view and the stone surround. Once the paint is dry, remove the masking tape.

1 **PAINTING THE WINDOW IN PERSPECTIVE**
Finally, add the open leaded-glass window. Trace the template on page 135, then position the design so that the top half ends in the middle, and with a gap about 2.5cm (1in) on the right between the window and frame, to allow for the hinges and thicker leading. Tape to secure, and slide carbon paper underneath.

2 Re-trace the lines with a pencil and ruler, then reverse the same tracing, line it up in the middle and trace in the lower half of the window in the same way. The whole window is then ready to paint.

3 Use the pencil lines as a guide for painting the window leading. First, place a strip of 'Magic™ Tape' on either side of the diamond pattern, leaving a strip 6mm (¼in) in width, for the leading. Then mix a dark grey paint, and paint in the leading with a soft, flat size 4 artists' brush. Be systematic and paint the centre panels first, followed by the surrounding longer shapes.

4 Make the outside edge of the window extra thick, to allow for the hinges that will be added in the next stage.

5 Add extra width to the leading by painting a lighter shade of grey to the right of all dark lines. Finally, paint in the hinges.

Detail of a hinge

1 **PAINTING THE STAINED GLASS**
Next paint the stained glass. Start with ultramarine blue, thinning the paint with clean water, to make it very dilute. (Clean water is essential, to ensure the colour remains pure and translucent.) As the paint is so thin, work on a flat surface to avoid it running.

Before it dries, wipe away some of the paint in the centre, with a finger inside a clean cloth. This renders the paint more transparent, while leaving a build-up of colours in the corners, mimicking the effect of genuine coloured glass.

Repeat the technique, using cadmium red for alternate sections.

1 FINISHING TOUCHES

I have added touches that reinforce the trompe l'oeil effect, give a sense of perspective to the painting and entice the viewer to look closer: I placed a purple emperor butterfly, copied from a book, on the stone surround and another smaller yellow butterfly on the window frame.

There are many different species of butterfly – you could choose a particular colour that appeals, or perhaps a butterfly that is common to your area.

2

Finally, add depth to the sill by painting a thicker line in a lighter tone on the top edge of the stone, and a window stay with a curled end, to create an attractive and decorative shadow across the stonework.

MEMO BOARD

with trompe l'oeil letters and memorabilia

Trompe l'oeil memo boards were popular in the seventeenth century, particularly among the Dutch Masters who excelled in the realistic depiction of notes, letters and other memorabilia, attached by pins and ribbons across a board. The ribbon or tape is fixed crisscross style to the wood panel, a geometric arrangement which defines the composition. Letters and memorabilia painted by the artist may have lost their meaning now, but are imbued with a lost significance of the everyday life of another time in history.

Select items that have meaning and significance to you – a cherished note, or a quotation that amuses, an addressed envelope – to form the 'still life' of this project. For the example shown here, I chose a gardening theme and so gathered some of the everyday items of a gardener: a postcard, a seed packet, a label with string, a plant marker and a gardening glove. Whatever items you choose, you can follow the guidelines below.

The board is made from a square of MDF. If possible get a woodworker to finish the edges with a router, as this will form a decorative edge and the board will not require additional framing.

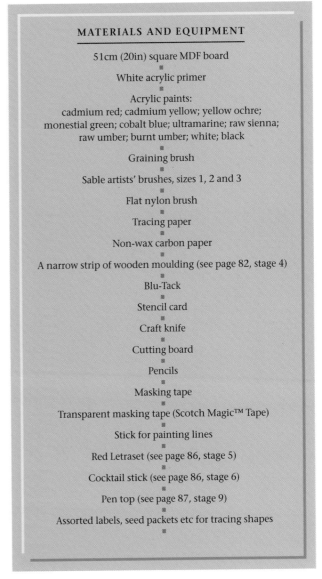

MATERIALS AND EQUIPMENT

51cm (20in) square MDF board

White acrylic primer

Acrylic paints:
cadmium red; cadmium yellow; yellow ochre; monestial green; cobalt blue; ultramarine; raw sienna; raw umber; burnt umber; white; black

Graining brush

Sable artists' brushes, sizes 1, 2 and 3

Flat nylon brush

Tracing paper

Non-wax carbon paper

A narrow strip of wooden moulding (see page 82, stage 4)

Blu-Tack

Stencil card

Craft knife

Cutting board

Pencils

Masking tape

Transparent masking tape (Scotch Magic™ Tape)

Stick for painting lines

Red Letraset (see page 86, stage 5)

Cocktail stick (see page 86, stage 6)

Pen top (see page 87, stage 9)

Assorted labels, seed packets etc for tracing shapes

 Templates for the tulip and the lettering are on pages 136 and 137.

1 PREPARING THE BOARD

Prepare the board by painting with two coats of acrylic primer, allowing it to dry and sanding down between coats. When the second coat is dry, mix burnt umber and yellow ochre, dilute to the consistency of thin cream, add a little scumble glaze, and apply with a one inch brush. 'Brush out' with a grainer while still damp, then allow to dry.

3 Add more monestial green to the mixture, to make a richer shade of green and apply it, with a narrower, dry brush, just to the outer edges of the panel; drag the paint down in vertical strokes, but allow the 'wood' tones to still show through.

2 Next, dilute some green and raw umber with water (to single cream consistency again), add a touch of scumble glaze for transparency, then apply this over the previous colour. To give the surface depth and character, vary the application of the paint so that areas of the previous brown 'wood' colour show through slightly. Brush out as before, with the graining brush, then leave to dry.

4 Next, rule lines to indicate the individual planks of wood. Add some black to the green mixture and dilute to make it slightly runny, so that the paint flows easily. To paint the lines, rest the metal part of the paintbrush on a piece of wooden moulding and drag the loaded brush downwards. When dry, paint another line abutting the first, in the same way, but this time using white paint with a touch of green and raw umber.

1 ADDING THE RIBBON AND MEMORABILIA

Rule in 1cm (⅜in) wide strips for the ribbon, in a crisscross shape within a square. Mask off the square, then paint it in with cadmium red and a touch of white. To simulate tension, add more white and yellow ochre to the red, and blend this lighter shade in the centre of each ribbon, using a flat brush.

2 Once dry, tape the middle section in the same way and paint in the crisscross arrangement in the centre.

TIP

If your shapes are too complex for the tape to follow, paint to the outline with a fine brush and fill in with a larger brush.

3 Position the items you have chosen to depict on the flat memo board and, once you are happy with the composition, fix them in place with Blu-Tack and draw around them. Before painting, mask around the edges of each outline with 'Magic™ Tape' and mask over the ribbon to protect it. This will ensure a neat finish around the edge and protect the areas already painted. 'Block in' the masked-off areas with white paint, applying a second coat if necessary. Allow to dry.

4 Pencil a rectangle, 6mm (¼in) in from the outside edge of the postcard, to form a white border; mask off this border and paint the postcard and label with a buff colour, mixed from burnt umber and white. Once dry, remove the tape from around the shapes, but leave the tape protecting the ribbon in place until the detail has been built up (see page 87).

5 Trace the tulip from the template (see page 136), and position the tracing on the buff postcard, top right; slide carbon paper underneath and re-trace.

Use the same method for tracing the lettering of your choice (see lettering template on page 137). I chose a flower name and the lettering used adds a decorative calligraphic flourish.

1 **APPLYING THE COLOUR DETAILS**
Now add the colour. First paint the lettering in raw umber, using a fine brush; graphics on the plant marker in blue; then the stem and leaf of the tulip and the background green on the seed packet, in monestial green. Shape the bulk of the glove by blending dark grey at the edges with white, keeping darker shades to left-hand side.

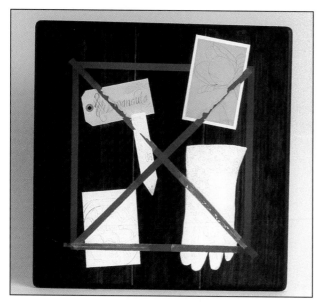

6 Trace the design from your chosen seed packet and transfer to the memo board using the method described above. Pencil in areas of fabric and the fingers of the gardening glove.

2 Build up a little more detail on each item: a wash of raw umber on the label to simulate age; more graphics on the plant marker; a yellow ochre glaze on the tulip (to add colour without obscuring the drawing); pink glaze to the inside of the flower shapes and the fabric design on the glove.

3 To add further shape to the tulip, apply another coat of yellow ochre around the foreground petal. Deepen the flowers on the seed packet and pick out a second colour on the pattern of the glove fabric.

5 Add further detail to the tulip, painting the foreground petals with a brighter yellow and the tip of the leaf with a paler yellow-green. Next, use red Letraset for the seed packet, to give it that printed graphic look. Just press the required letters on top of the finished artwork then, when the lettering is complete, apply a coat of matt or silk varnish to seal it.

4 Pencil in the label string, then paint it in using a size 1 sable brush. Noting detail from the actual item, add tiny specks of paint to emulate scuffing or soil on the pointed end of the plant marker, and red stripes on the tulip, applying a darker red to the foreground markings. Paint in the blue flowers on the glove.

6 To print the 'rubber' dots on the glove, use a cocktail stick with the pointed end sliced off. First, lightly pencil in diagonal lines on the glove as a guide, then mix a quantity of paint, load a brush with it, and press the stick first into the brush, then onto the area to be printed.

7 Once the paint is dry, remove the masking tape covering the ribbons and your objects will appear to be held in place behind the them. Tape around the ribbons again and paint the lower edge a brighter shade of red.

8 Now add some little touches which will make the trompe l'oeil even more effective: apply shadow – using a mix of raw umber and scumble glaze – to the glove and seed packet immediately below the ribbon, then give the tulip postcard a curled corner, by painting a very narrow line of raw umber along the 'fold'. When dry, apply the same colour over the corner as a wash, intensifying the colour down towards the fold.

9 Next add the drawing pins that keep the ribbons in place: I used a pen top to print a dark brown circle of colour, then carefully filled in to the edges with yellow ochre. As a finishing touch, print a yellow-white highlight on the top left corner of each pin, using the cocktail stick.

10 Next, paint in the shadows that fall across the wooden planking, using a mixture of black, green and raw umber. Start approximately 12mm (½in) from the right-hand side of each item, and paint up to their edges, following their shapes. Finally, thin out the edges with water, to give the shapes a soft outline, and your board is complete.

ORIENTAL CUPBOARD

with Chinese plate, cup, books and a vase of flowers

Gold stencilling creates an opulent framework around the rich red of this trompe l'oeil oriental cupboard and the oriental theme continues with the Chinese willow pattern decorating the plate and cup, the detail on the book spine and the motif on the lace-edged cloth. An antique vase, filled with flowers inside the dark mahogany interior, adds a final touch to the design.

A kitchen door panel is ideal for this project as it is easily purchased and precise size is not important – it will only need a couple of coats of primer and you are then ready to start.

Templates are included for the blue willow pattern designs on the plate and the cup, the book outlines, the vase of flowers, the decorations and the lace edging. If you prefer to choose your own objects for the cupboard, photograph them, trace them and enlarge on a photocopier if necessary, using the stencils provided as a guidance for size; then transfer them to the cupboard (see stage 1, page 92). You could also personalize the books, by tracing the lettering or designs on books of special importance to you.

MATERIALS AND EQUIPMENT

Wooden kitchen door panel

White acrylic primer

Sandpaper

Graining brush

Acrylic paints:
burnt umber
raw umber
raw sienna
yellow ochre
cadmium red
cadmium yellow
cobalt blue
ultramarine blue
black
white
monestial green
purple
'antique' gold in tube

Scumble glaze

Sable artists' brush, size 1 or 2

Palette

Stencil card

Small stencil brush

Compass

Masking tape

Craft knife

Cutting board

Carbon paper

Ruler

Pencil

White chinagraph pencil

Permanent gold marker pen (see page 96, stage 7)

Acrylic varnish (satin and 'dead flat')

 Templates for cupboard decoration and contents on pages 138–41.

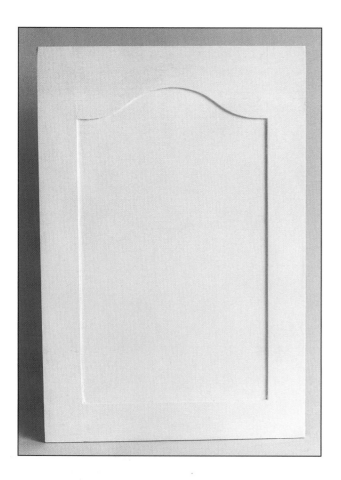

1 PAINTING THE CUPBOARD

Apply two coats of primer to the panel, allowing the paint to dry and sanding down between coats.

2

Next, dilute some yellow ochre with a little water, and apply this over the primer. When dry, mix some burnt umber and raw umber to make a rich dark brown, thin with water, then add a little scumble glaze (for translucency) and apply this all over the panel. Apply a graining brush or wide bristle brush to the paint while still damp, using vertical brush strokes to simulate the grain of the wood.

Pay special attention to the centre of the panel, which will form the back of the cupboard and be more visible, and make sure the yellow ochre still shows through this dark brown glaze. Allow to dry for at least two hours before continuing with the next stage.

3

Next, paint the cupboard frame. To define the area, measure 12mm (½in) in from the edges of the centre panel and rule a pencilled line around. Protect the inner panel with masking tape, following the pencilled line and bunching the tape up for the upper curved edge. Apply a coat of cadmium red to the frame, leave to dry for 20 minutes, then apply a second coat.

4 To decorate the frame, first mark the centre of the top, bottom, and sides of the panel. Trace the templates for the motifs (see page 138) onto stencil card, then cut them out. For the bottom and side decorations ('A'), cut just the central flower motif and one half of the design, then secure the stencil in position with masking tape, placing the flower on the centre mark. Squeeze some gold paint onto a palette and press the stencil brush into the paint – it should not need any thinning with water – then stencil on the design. To complete the design, remove and pat dry the stencil, then reverse and reposition it over the central flower motif. Repeat the process with motif 'B'.

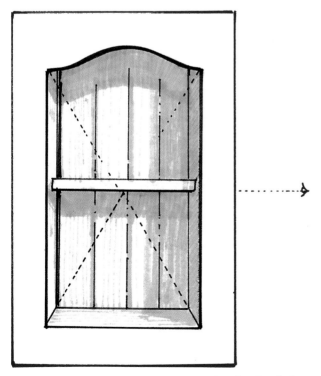

Dotted lines indicate the vanishing point for the shelves

5 Next, paint the cupboard interior. To find the correct angle for the bottom shelf, join up the four corners of the cupboard with a cross, using the chinagraph pencil, then draw a horizontal line between these angles. Now draw an inner rectangle to represent the depth of the cupboard, 4cm (1½in) from the top and sides, and 5cm (2in) from the bottom, and draw the lines in with the chinagraph pencil. Paint them – and the 'plank' lines at the back – with a mixture of raw umber and a touch of black. To create the illusion of depth between the outer frame and the interior, paint a shadow below the red curved top and on the right-hand side, using a wash of raw umber and black.

6 Mark the position of the shelf roughly in the middle of the cupboard, making it 2.5cm (1in) thick. Mask off the area and paint it with cadmium red to match the outer cupboard. Once dry, paint in a shadow below the shelf, using a mix of raw umber and black, and blending the edges to merge with the wooden planking.

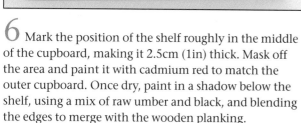

TIP

While the paint is still wet, soften the shadows with an oblong stippling brush. Use the brush horizontally, and stipple the paint downwards, so that the shadows are blended into the planking.

1 **THE OBJECTS IN THE CUPBOARD**
Sketch in the objects in the cupboard, using the chinagraph pencil. The templates provided (on pages 138–41) can be used in outline, or your own designs can be sketched in (see introductory text).

2 Block in the shapes with white paint, painting carefully up to the outlined edge. Fill in with a larger flat brush, allow to dry, then apply a second coat if necessary. Once this is dry, trace the designs, and transfer them using carbon paper.

3 Before starting on the detail, paint shading on the left hand side of the cup using a pale blue/grey, mixed from ultramarine, black and white. Blend the colour into the white of the cup, so that the shape takes on the roundness of the cup. While this is drying, use a size 2 sable brush to paint in the design on the plate, using quite thin ultramarine blue. Paint a first coat on the spines of the books – don't worry if, at this stage, they look a little patchy – and paint the vase with a dark grey, leaving some highlights unpainted on the right. Begin to colour in the flowers.

4 Progress with more detail: complete the design on the cup, add more paint to the book spines, adding lighter colour on the right hand side, to indicate the curve of the spine. Add more colours to the flowers. Draw your chosen design on the vase, then paint in the design with a flat brown undercoat. Pick out areas across the top of the design in yellow, to simulate gold highlights.

5 Complete the basic book spines, using a mixture of raw umber and black for the shadows down their left sides, and white for highlights.

6 Pencil in the outline of the shadow cast by the cup, following the concave surface of the plate. For the shadow, use a mix of ultramarine, a little purple and black softened with white, and a touch of scumble glaze to make the paint translucent; this translucency is important, to ensure the design on the plate is not obscured. Draw in bands, and the lettering and decoration of your choice, across the spines of the books – I have used yellow ochre, to look like gold, for one book and outlined a Japanese face in black to decorate the book on oriental art. To make the foreground of the bottom shelf stand out, paint with a mixture of yellow ochre and white, blending the colours into the dark recesses at the back. Paint the left hand side panel of the cupboard with the same colour, to define the space between the side panel and the blue book.

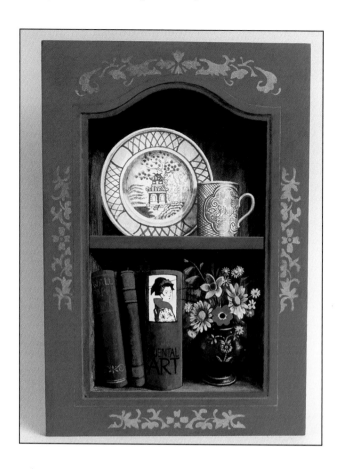

7 Next, the highlight on the right-hand side of the cup: fix masking tape to ensure an even line, then stipple in a band of white paint thinned with scumble glaze and water. Remove the tape, then soften the edges.

With a gold pen and a ruler, draw a line 2cm (¾in) wide on the inner edge of the red frame, to contain the border design.

8 Trace the border from template 'C', on page 139, then transfer to the frame, as shown. Use the gold pen to draw in the zig zag shapes first, then the narrower lines in alternate directions. If you wish to add a lace-edged cloth, as I have done, trace the design from the template (on page 138), then check the length of the shelf before positioning the tracing: I was able to repeat the design four times. Position the motif with a piece of tape, slide under a small piece of carbon paper and retrace the design.

9 Using a sable brush, size 1 or 2, carefully paint in the lace design with slightly diluted white paint. A good 'point' on the end of your brush will ensure crisp marks to imitate the fine strands of lacy cotton. You will find the lace cloth immediately gives a spatial effect to the painting – the shelf comes forward and the objects sit back happily.

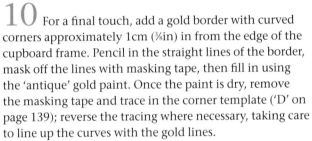

10 For a final touch, add a gold border with curved corners approximately 1cm (⅜in) in from the edge of the cupboard frame. Pencil in the straight lines of the border, mask off the lines with masking tape, then fill in using the 'antique' gold paint. Once the paint is dry, remove the masking tape and trace in the corner template ('D' on page 139); reverse the tracing where necessary, taking care to line up the curves with the gold lines.

11 The painting is now complete but, to emphasize the trompe l'oeil effect, varnish the red and gold frame with satin varnish, and the cupboard interior with dead flat varnish.

TROMPE L'OEIL FRESCO

inspired by Greek wall paintings

A fresco is a painting executed directly onto wet plaster walls, a method much favoured by the Greeks and Romans. Some frescoes are hundreds of years old and the bright colours have become faded and the plaster pitted and crumbling – the texture caused by the passage of time that we find so appealing. This fresco design, depicting a dancing scene, is influenced by the beautiful murals in Tuscany which still survive, despite being painted as long ago as 470BC.

This project describes how to create crumbling plaster textures and faded painted colour effects with foam and 'sheepskin' rollers. I painted this fresco design on an external corner wall with a rough surface, which is perfect for creating an authentic-looking crumbling fresco. For this area, 2.1m x 4.5m (7ft high x 15ft wide) – about 9.5 sq m (100 sq ft) – it is more economical to buy paints ready mixed from a DIY store. I chose 'seashell pink', a brand name paint, for the wall and refer to it as the 'base colour'. Two other basic colours – 'terracotta', and a cool 'stone' shade – are also used. I have included acrylic paints in the project, because they mix easily with these three basic colours and will broaden the range of colours. When dry, these paints are waterproof and will not 'run'.

There are many templates which provide the basic shapes to be copied, including the 1.2m (4ft) high figures, as well as designs to be made into stencils, such as the decorative borders which run above and below the dancing figures.

 Templates for figures on pages 142–3, and for designs on pages 144–6.

1 PREPARING THE WALL

Wash down the wall surface, using a stiff bristle brush, warm water and sugar soap then, using a spirit level, rule straight horizontal lines to establish the area to be painted. Mask off the area before painting.

2 Apply the 'seashell' base coat, a muted shade of pink, with a fluffy roller. When dry, apply another coat.

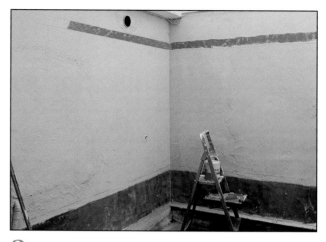

3 Measure 45cm (18in) up from your base line, then use your spirit level and ruler to ensure a straight and level line for the border. Measure another line 7.5cm (3in) from the base line – this 38cm (15in) space between the ruled lines will form the lower border.

Mask off the border edges, then, using a fluffy roller and the 'terracotta' paint, apply the paint, varying the direction of the roller, so that the base coat still shows through in parts. Leave the masking tape in place, and darken the terracotta tone with raw umber and black, then apply this with a clean fluffy roller. The 'open' imprint of the roller allows the previous colours to show through and a richly textured effect can be created effortlessly in this way. Once the paint is dry, remove the masking tape.

Measure another 7.5cm (3in) border 23cm (9in) from the top edge and mask this off. Use the same method with the fluffy roller, allowing the base coat to show through. Once the paint is dry, remove the masking tape.

4 For the next coat, use the customized foam roller. Apply a ready-mixed 'stone' paint with this – quite randomly – over the base coat and top border, to give the 'distressed' look of crumbling plaster.

1 ADDING THE FIGURES

Next, draw the grid for the figures on the wall, using a long ruler and spirit level. Each figure is four 30cm (1ft) squares high, by three 30cm (1ft) squares wide, so will be approximately 1.2m high by 90cm wide (4 x 3ft). The grids on the figure templates on pages 142 and 143 will help you scale the figures up, as each 5cm (2in) square on the template corresponds to the larger 30cm (1ft) squares drawn on the wall.

2 Draw the figures on the wall, copying the grid square by square. Start with the simpler outlines, and gradually build up the shape by adding the smaller details.

3 Charcoal in the fall of a curtain and a large urn on the right of the mural, to add balance to the composition, and 'frame' the design.

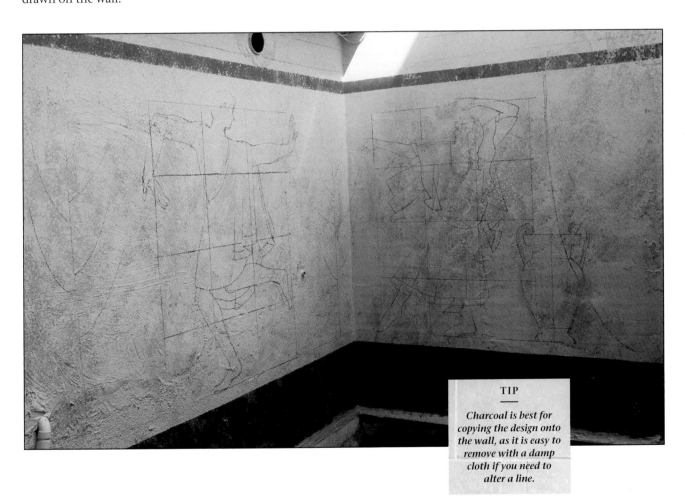

TIP

Charcoal is best for copying the design onto the wall, as it is easy to remove with a damp cloth if you need to alter a line.

4 Once the basic design is charcoaled in, paint over the outlines with a free, spontaneous line using diluted terracotta paint and a size 8 tapered paintbrush.

5 When the outlines are complete, take a larger brush and block in the tunic and sleeves of the female dancer with 'terracotta' paint. Paint the curtain with the same colour, but this time apply it with a small roller. Just using the edge of the roller to indicate the folds is an easy way to blend the colour: place some paint in a roller tray then, holding the roller at an angle, apply paint to half the sleeve only. Use the roller flat to apply the colour, following the pencilled line of the folds.

6 Add raw umber to the 'terracotta', to produce a darker tone, and use the customized roller to apply this around the curved edges at the bottom of the curtain. Leave the base coat showing through in parts, to add texture. Next, paint the folds in the skirt, again using just the edge of a small roller. Draw a band in for the skirt, and infill with cobalt blue.

7 Mix flesh tones, using 'terracotta', 'seashell' pink and a touch of yellow ochre. To create roundness, keep the colour darker at the outlines and add white to blend to a lighter tone at the centre. Block in the vase with black, using a small roller, and the tunic of the male dancer with cobalt blue mixed with white. To create a subtle contrast among the folds around the hemline, add black or raw umber to the cobalt paint to darken it. To indicate the position of the foliage stem, draw a vertical charcoal line, then draw smaller stems outwards from this. Sketch in the handles on the urn.

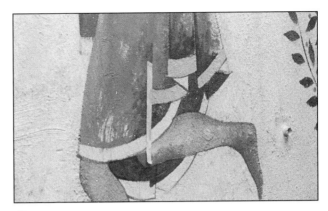

1 THE BACKGROUND DETAILS

Mix a mid-green from fairly dilute monestial green, yellow and white, and paint the stems of the bushes with this, tapering the stems by gradually lifting the end of the brush as you paint. Make a single leaf stencil from the template on page 144 and print leaves either side of each branch to build up the foliage. Stencil large cadmium red dots or 'berries' among the leaves. Paint in the hair of the dancers, with burnt umber and 'terracotta' and add black for shading. Gradually complete the detail of the figures and paint the curved handles on the urn.

2

Paint in the hem of the blue tunic with a blend of yellow and yellow ochre. If the texture of the wall is uneven, you can mask off the hem before painting, to ensure a neat edge.

3

Use the templates on page 144 as a guide to copy, or enlarge and trace, the outlines of the birds, then paint in their bodies using white, pale blue and pink. Next, use a spirit level to draw in a light charcoal line for the 'egg and dart' pattern, about 10cm (4in) above the red border. Make an egg and dart stencil by enlarging the template on page 144 to fit the width of your border. Fix the stencil in place with masking tape and use a stencil brush to paint in the blue shapes with a mix of cobalt blue and white.

> ### TIP
> ---
> *To print an even and continuous line, when stencilling egg and dart pattern, overlap the last printed shape with the first stencil as you progress from right to left.*

4 Now decorate the lower border. Although frescoes appear to be freehand, repeating complex shapes is actually much easier if you use a stencil. Trace the templates on page 145, adjusting and overlapping the shapes to make one complete 's' shape. Repeat the process to make another reversed or 'mirrored' stencil and stencil in the design using the 'seashell' base coat.

While the lower border is drying, use the egg and dart stencil again – locating the position over the printed blue shapes – to print the cadmium red loops. Hand paint the gaps afterwards, applying the same colour with a brush. Sketch in a blackbird, perched on the urn, and a charcoal line to represent the floor. It will be easier to paint the line if you mask off a 12mm (½in) band along the charcoal line and infill with cadmium red, using a small roller or paintbrush.

5 Complete the lower border with the 'sprouting leaves' template on page 146. To ensure the stem of the stencil is centrally placed between the two 's' shapes, mark the centre point with charcoal or white chalk and locate through the stencil before printing. Join up the gaps with a paintbrush afterwards.

To add movement and rhythm to the dancing scene, charcoal in some long stems of foliage, growing upwards from the red line, then hand paint them in green. Next, fill in the blackbird: dip a dry paintbrush in neat black paint, wipe off the excess, then stipple in the paint, allowing the base coat to remain visible.

> ### NOTE
>
> *In order to make the border templates less fragile, I have left small sections of stencil paper running across the stencil, over areas to be painted. Once the design has been stencilled in, and the stencil itself removed, it is a simple matter to hand-paint over the telltale gaps with the same colour, to complete the design.*

6 Use the larger 'leaf' template on page 144 to make a stencil to print leaves growing outwards from the stems and smaller hand-painted leaves near the black urn on the right. Decorate the urn as shown, if you wish, with smaller figures and a looped line running straight across the widest part.

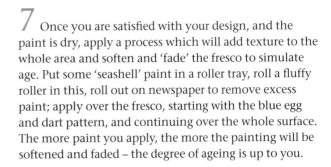

7 Once you are satisfied with your design, and the paint is dry, apply a process which will add texture to the whole area and soften and 'fade' the fresco to simulate age. Put some 'seashell' paint in a roller tray, roll a fluffy roller in this, roll out on newspaper to remove excess paint; apply over the fresco, starting with the blue egg and dart pattern, and continuing over the whole surface. The more paint you apply, the more the painting will be softened and faded – the degree of ageing is up to you.

8 To make the fresco even more convincing, add some trompe l'oeil 'cracks'. To do this, mark a 'wandering' line with a stick of charcoal, then paint the line with medium grey paint, opening up the shape to indicate broader cracks. Follow this with a white line, abutting the 'opened up' shape, but just to the right of it, on the actual fresco. This will add depth to the top surface, which will appear to have fallen away, revealing the plaster underneath. Finally, add a thin – almost black – line on the right hand side to define the broken edge of the fresco and your mural is complete.

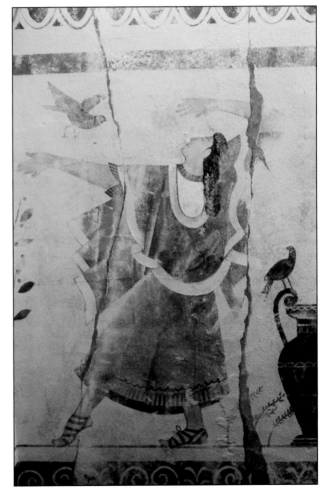

MURAL DESIGN
room with a trompe l'oeil view

While on holiday in France I took this photograph of a window in a quiet country village, and it has inspired me to paint several trompe l'oeil versions since. I have used artistic licence of course, as my design is for an indoor window looking out across the countryside. The postcards and letters are different in each painting, to reflect the personality and tastes of an individual. As the painting will be life-size, you need a wall over 1.65m (5ft 6in) in width and 2.1m (7ft) in height – mine was a plain plastered interior wall. I used matt paint for the base coat, to avoid reflections which might spoil the illusion.

MATERIALS

Sugar soap and sponge

2½ litre (half gallon) can 'county cream' vinyl matt emulsion

50mm (2in) brush to apply base colour

Acrylic paints:
cobalt blue
white
purple
yellow ochre,
cadmium yellow
cadmium red
monestial green
raw umber
burnt umber
black
white

Small pots for mixing colours

Small foam roller

Roller painting tray

Graining brush

Plastic palette knife

Masking tape

1m (3ft) ruler or retractable metallic tape measure

Spirit level

Oblong stippling brush

Stencil card

Craft knife

Cutting board

Dead flat acrylic varnish

Templates for hinges, postcard, flowers and heart on pages 147–8; shutters on pages 149.

1 Wash the wall down with a sponge and sugar soap. When dry, apply two coats of cream paint with a foam roller, allowing it to dry between coats.

2 Once the base coat is dry, draw in the design. Measure the length of your wall, halve the measurement to find the centre of the window and mark this point with a pencil. Draw in the window frame. Establish the width of the top edge by measuring 38cm (15in) either side of the centre, and mark these points with a pencil. Next, measure 2.1m (7ft) up from the ground and, using a spirit level, draw a horizontal line between the two marked points. Now measure down 113cm (45in) from this line and, using the spirit level again, draw another horizontal line to establish the bottom edge of the window frame.

You should now have a window measuring 113cm high by 75cm wide (45 x 30in). Do check at this stage that your lines are correct – the easiest way is to stand back and compare levels that are drawn to those that exist in the room. Don't worry about pencil marks at this stage – they can be rubbed out or painted over.

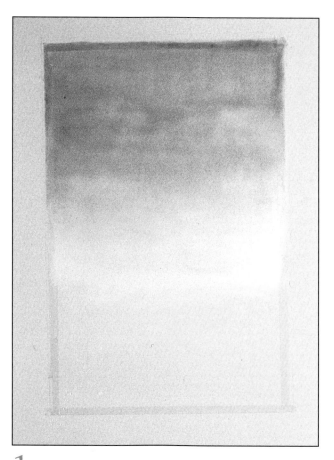

1 **PAINTING THE LANDSCAPE**
Place masking tape around the window frame to ensure a clean edge to the painting, then start with the sky. Mix a medium blue from cobalt and white – a third of a jam jar will be sufficient – and pour some of it into another jar. Add a dollop of scumble glaze to lengthen drying time and to help blend the colours. Start painting at the top of the frame, gradually paling the colour to almost white two thirds of the way down. Remember, the colour must change gradually, from deep to pale, to create the feeling of depth. While the paint is still wet, use the oblong stippling brush and, starting from the top, stipple methodically across from left to right, blending the shades of blue into each other. This will remove any residual hard colour divisions and brush marks, and complete the tonal change from blue to white.

2 Pencil in a 'wandering' line for the distant mountain range, then pour a little of the ready-mixed mid-blue into a palette and add sufficient purple paint to make a warm blue/lilac shade. If this seems too dark when applied, add more white paint. Keep the colours pale, so they merge and the shapes are not defined – you are aiming for an impression of a landscape, rather than a perfectly clear photographic style.

3 Apply paint horizontally across the picture, working downwards as you do so and gradually introduce more colour. Mix a blue-green shade by adding a very small amount of monestial green to the mixed mid-blue and paint an uneven line of this colour across the picture, approximately 5cm (2in) deep below the mountain range. Work it into the previous colour to merge the edges and, if it seems too dark when applied, add white.

4 Next, mix a pale greeny-yellow by adding about 1cm (⅜in) of yellow from a tube to the jam jar containing the palest blue. Apply this as a band of colour, as shown on the right, allowing some of the background base coat of cream to show through in parts.

5 Finally, apply darker green towards the bottom strip of masking tape. For this, add a quarter teaspoon of monestial green and a touch of yellow to the previous colour, to darken it. When you are satisfied with your 'view' remove the masking tape. You will find the overall effect is one of space and of colour gradually merging into the distance.

1 **ADDING THE WINDOW FRAMES**
Now add the window frames, starting with the single closed frame on the left: first draw a straight line down the centre of your 'view' to mark the outer edge of the left-hand frame. Then measure an inner rectangle, 5cm (2in) in from the defined space, to represent the width of the frame and mask off the frame for painting.

2 For the window frame colour, mix burnt umber with ultramarine blue, then adjust the colour with white until you achieve a medium shade of brown. Mix enough paint for both frames – about half a teacup in total – and pour it into a roller painting tray. Apply the paint with a small foam roller – a quick and simple method that will minimize the risk of paint 'bleeding' under the masking tape. Then add some white paint to the previously mixed brown – to make a paler shade – and apply this with a graining brush, dragging it over the surface to imitate the grain of wood.

3 The window frame is opened outwards towards the landscape. This makes the frame appear elongated, because it is seen in perspective, so the width of the open frame should be just over half the width of the closed one (see diagram 1).

Measure from the right-hand side of the open frame, mark the width with a pencil, then use a spirit level to draw the straight vertical line. Now measure approximately 10cm (4in) down this vertical line and join this point with the top right-hand corner to achieve the angle of the open window, and measure up 10cm (4in) from the bottom of the window to find the correct angle there. Stand back some distance and look at the shape you have drawn – it is easy to alter the pencil lines at this stage.

Refer to diagram 2 for the inner shape. The wood frame has been drawn less than 5cm (2in) thick at its furthest point, and more than 5cm (2in) thick at the nearest vertical line, because we are seeing the inner edge. Once the shape has been established, mask off the frame and apply the previously mixed brown paint as before.

Leave to dry, then remove the masking tape.

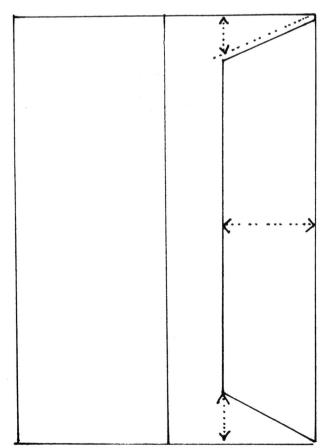

Diagram 1

Diagram 2

4 To create the depth of the window reveal, measure 5cm (2in) outwards from the sides and the top edge of the window, and 7.5cm (3in) from the bottom to allow extra depth for the sill; pencil in, joining the corner points diagonally to add the perspective to each corner. Mask off the top and right hand reveals, which are in shadow, and paint these with a very dilute mix of ultramarine and raw umber, using a dry brush. Next, mask off the lower sill, and loosely paint in a creeping shadow, to suggest depth. Blend the colour along the sill, working towards the left, so the shadow fades out gently – using a round stippling brush will help to soften the hard edge. Apply white paint, thinned but not runny, along the left of the sill and on the masked-off, left-hand reveal. Remove the masking tape and you will see that the shape and space are gradually becoming more three dimensional.

1 **THE PINK SHUTTERS**
Next pencil in the shutters. Make each one 40cm wide x 117cm tall (16 x 46in) and place them 4cm (1½in) out from the painted reveals.

Mask off the outlines and prepare the colour. Half fill a small container with white paint; add 12mm (½in) of cadmium red from the tube and mix with a palette knife, then 6mm (¼in) of yellow, to make salmon pink. Add

water to make a thin cream consistency and adjust the amounts of paint if you prefer paler (more white) or brighter pink (more red). As this is a fairly large area, use a broad brush to block the shapes and simulate the effect of grain. One coat will be enough – don't worry if the base coat is seen in patches; this colour will be the base for the next stage, so leave masking tape in place.

2 When both shutters have been painted in, apply some graining. Mix a darker pink, using some of the previous colour plus a little more cadmium red and raw umber (the same amount of each); dilute slightly with water and apply with a graining brush, dragging downwards to simulate wood grain. Work from top to bottom, covering each section methodically from left to right – the lines don't have to be particularly straight, as wood grain varies in pattern (see pages 22–3). Leave to dry.

3 Divide each shutter into three equally spaced vertical 'planks' of wood, and rule in pencilled guidelines. Paint in the lines with a very dilute dark brown paint, mixed by adding more raw umber to the previous colour. Use a fine tapered brush and a spirit level to guide your hand as you paint the lines.

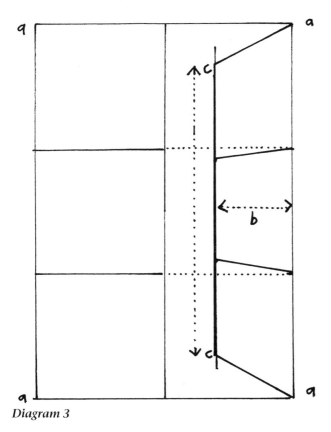

Diagram 3

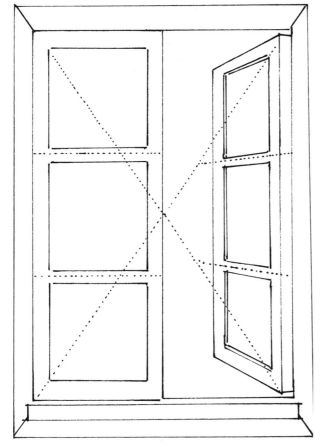

Diagram 4

4 Next, you can add a simple but effective 'heart' decoration to each shutter. Make a stencil of the template on page 148 and stencil hearts onto the shutters, making sure they are level. Stipple in the heart shape using the cream base coat, which will give the illusion of seeing through to the wall behind.

5 To find the position of the glazing bars, divide the closed window into three equal parts (see diagram 3, above). Mark these divisions with pencil lines, then mask off a strip about 12mm (½in) either side of the line and paint in the bars to match the rest of the window (see diagram 4, to the left, and also page 110, stage 1).

To calculate the angle of the glazing bars on the open window, divide the inner height of the right hand side of the window into three and mark these points; repeat the process on the shorter left hand side, then join the two sides up. Stand back to check that the angles look right, then mask off the bars, and paint in, as previously.

1 ADDING THE DETAILS

Use the template on page 147 to make a stencil for the decorative metal hinges. First, pencil in horizontal centre lines on the outer 'planks' of each shutter, roughly quarter of the way down from the top and up from the bottom. Line these up with the centre of your stencil and fix it in place with masking tape. Mix some burnt umber and a little cadmium red to a nice, rusty red and apply this with a stencil or stippling brush. Keep the paint fairly dry, to stop any 'bleeding' under the stencil. Complete all four bracket ends, then hand-paint the 'gaps'.

2

Use the hinge stencil in the same way, lining up the middle of the stencil with your centre line. Join up the tapering sides of the stencil with masking tape, adjusting the length to your shutter width, then stencil in the rusty red. Hand-paint the gaps afterwards, as before. Use the same colour, and a small artists' brush, to paint the 'reveal' of the heart shape on the left, so that it looks as if it is cut into the wood. Use the heart shape edge of the stencil to help draw this line, and paint in with a small artists' brush. Paint the outer edge of the left hand shutter with the same colour, to create the thickness of the shutter.

3 PENCILLING IN THE SHAPES

Draw around your chosen shapes with a pencil, then mask them off. Here, two postcards are positioned on the right, and an airmail envelope on the left.

4 Block in the postcards with a pale pink and a pale blue, and use pale lilac for the envelope. Leave the masking tape in place while you vary the tones, to create the effect of undulations in the envelope paper, adding more blue to the lilac, to darken and more white to lighten areas within the envelope shape.

1 THE VASE OF FLOWERS

A vase of sunflowers on the window sill adds to the French theme. Enlarge the template on page 148 to approximately 38cm (15in) high, on a photocopier. (Photocopy directly onto A2 or A3 tracing paper if possible, as this will make it much easier to position the design.) Place the base of the vase carefully within the sill

area before securing the template with tape. Slide non-wax carbon paper underneath and trace the design through. Block in the vase outline with ultramarine blue, mellowed slightly with raw umber and a little white. Paint in the centres of the sunflowers with purple and a little black – if too dark or contrasty lighten with a touch of white paint.

2 Once the paint is dry, re-position the tracing over the painting to draw in the petals of the sunflowers, then paint in the petals with golden or cadmium yellow. With a smaller brush, define the shapes of the petals using yellow ochre and a touch of cadmium red.

CREATING THE ILLUSION OF THE SHADOW ACROSS THE WINDOW SILL

A Draw in the outline of the shadow cast by the vase of flowers, using the illustration as reference.

B Fix masking tape along the top edge of the windowsill, then mix half a teacup or so of soft mauve for the shadow, from raw umber, ultramarine blue, purple and white. The paint should not be 'runny', so wipe any excess paint from brush on a newspaper or rag. Paint in the shadow shape on the sill down to the masking tape, then leave to dry. Save surplus paint for later use.

C Remove the tape to reveal a neat edge, then paint in the whole shadow area with the same mixture; this will darken the shadow already painted and soften the line of the sill. The cast shadow will now appear to follow the contours of the sill, creating a three-dimensional illusion. (Save the paint mixture, as it will be needed later for the shutter shadows.)

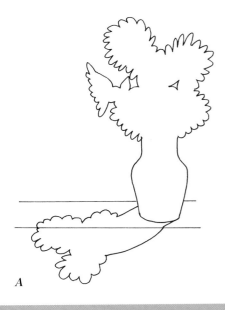

A

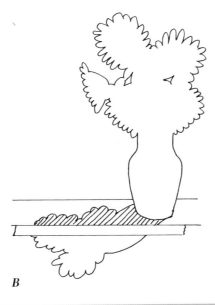

B

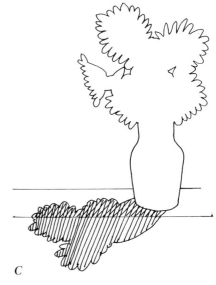

C

Detail of the original postcard

The painted postcard

Leave the masking tape in place until the details of the postcards are finished

PAINTING THE POSTCARDS

You can trace your own designs for the postcards, but you might like to use the flower template on page 139. Primulas are one of my favourite flowers and the detailed illustration on the facing page will help you to paint the flowers accurately. The other postcard I used is from France and shows a checked tablecloth and bottles of wine. The change of scale involves using much smaller brushes but the unfussy shapes and clear outlines make painting them a pleasure.

1 For the shadows cast by the shutters, use the soft mauve saved from stage 'B', on page 117. First, mask off the bottom edges of the shutters, then paint in the shadows. For a softer line use a dryer brush on the outer edge of the cast shadow then, when the paint is dry, lightly sand over the surface – the painted shadow looks more realistic when worked into the wall surface this way.

(Continued on page 122.)

Shadows are added after masking tape has been removed around postcards and shutters

CREATING THE ILLUSION OF THE FRENCH POSTCARD

A Position the tracing paper over the postcard picture and trace the basic shapes, then place the tracing paper over the area to be painted. Use non-wax carbon paper between the surface and tracing and draw in just the foreground table area. Block in foreground with pale purple paint, then the background with pale grey. Apply freely, as this is the 'under-painting' area.

B Use a size 3 sable paintbrush to paint in the gingham cloth with thinned cadmium red, in stripes across and down to form the checked pattern. When dry, reposition the tracing and carbon paper and draw in the wine glass, bottles and shadows.

C Darken some cadmium red with purple, thin so the background will show through, then paint in the wine in the glass and bottle. With a size 1 sable brush outline the bottles with dark green paint, but fill in the taller bottle, thinning with water at the centre to allow the light background to show through. This creates a lighter shade of green and imitates coloured glass. With a pencil draw a line on the left to indicate a corner fold.

D Paint the labels with white paint, blending the edges with grey to create a curved effect. Add details on the label using a size 1 sable brush. Paint the stem of the wine glass with a medium shade of green, mixed from cadmium yellow and monestial green thinned with water. Use thinned purple to paint in the areas of cast shadow and paint on the right-hand side of the centre bottle, to create a rounded effect. With dark grey paint, paint along the pencilled-in fold, and then wash the colour upwards toward the corner, to suggest a shadow. Finally, with white paint, add the highlights to the glass, and both bottles, to give a three-dimensional rendering to the picture postcard.

2 To create the illusion of the postcards standing out from the shutters, carefully paint up to the edges of the cards, and soften the outer shape against the shutters with a watery brush.

1 THE FINAL DETAILS

Again use the soft mauve saved from stage B (page 117) to paint some wandering lines imitating cracks, down towards the floor, and up from the top edge of the frame to the ceiling. Then mix some of the base coat cream with a small amount of raw umber, thin the mixture and sponge over the 'cracks'. This will give character to the wall surface and make the cracks more convincing. Add more of the original cream base coat if you want to merge these areas into the flat wall colour.

2

If you wish to personalize your mural, add a simple ultramarine blue name plate. I have painted 'Maison 1' to complete the French influence.

Finally, if you want to protect your mural from finger marks, varnish the surface with a 'dead flat' varnish. This is preferable to a satin finish, which might destroy the trompe l'oeil illusion.

TEMPLATES

USING THE TEMPLATES

You can trace the templates straight from the book but, if you need to scale them up or down, it is easiest to photocopy them first onto A4 or A3 paper and then reduce or enlarge as required on the photocopier.

Next, place tracing paper over the photocopied image and carefully trace the design using a sharp HB or B pencil. The resultant image, on semi-transparent paper, can then be placed and positioned accurately on your painting surface.

Secure the tracing to the surface with masking tape, then slide a piece of non-wax carbon paper underneath and retrace the design with the pencil. Remove the tracing and carbon paper to reveal the image and you are ready to paint. If you need to redraw any part of the design, the tracing can be re-positioned at any time, provided the surface it is placed on is dry.

MAKING STENCILS FROM THE TEMPLATES

Two methods are described below: the standard method, using bought stencil card, makes a strong stencil that can be re-used. After use, the stencil can be wiped with a clean rag and left to dry naturally; any slight residue of paint left on the stencil will actually strengthen it. The alternative method is quick, easy and cheaper, but the stencils cannot be kept for re-use.

STANDARD METHOD

Tape some stencil card to your cutting mat and, using a sharp pencil, firmly trace the template design onto the card through non-wax carbon paper. Remove the tracing and carbon paper and cut out the stencil with a craft knife.

PRINTING STENCILS

The very first time you use a newly cut stencil, print it on newspaper. This will absorb excess paint from the stencil brush and avoid blobs and bleeding underneath the stencil when you print it on your chosen surface.

To print *in situ*, position the stencil and stipple on paint that has been very slightly diluted. If you are printing the same image several times, check underneath the stencil between printing and, if there is any excess paint, blot it on newspaper. Don't re-load the brush each time you print the same image – variation in depth of colour is part of the charm of a stencilled surface.

TIP

If you photocopy a template directly onto A3 or A4 tracing paper, it will eliminate the hand-drawing process from template to tracing.

NOTE

In order to make some templates less fragile, I have left small sections of stencil paper running across the stencil, over areas to be painted. Once the design has been stencilled in, and the stencil itself removed, it is a simple matter to hand-paint over the telltale gaps with the same colour, to complete the design.

MAKING QUICK AND EASY STENCILS FROM PHOTOCOPIED TEMPLATES

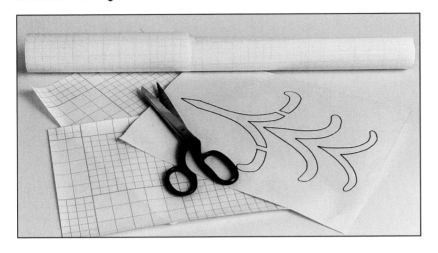

1 Cut two sheets of transparent Fablon or adhesive backing film (available from craft or hardware shops) to the same size as your template.

2 Remove the backing paper and cover both sides of the template with the film, pressing down firmly to remove air bubbles. The Fablon strengthens the paper, paint can be wiped off and the design is clearly visible to cut out, without having to retrace it.

3 Cut out the stencil, using a craft knife and cutting mat (see 'Tip' below).

TIP

When cutting stencil shapes, first secure the design to the mat with masking tape. Follow the template very carefully when cutting out the stencil and, for an accurate shape, press firmly and evenly, to ensure you cut right through the thickness of the card.

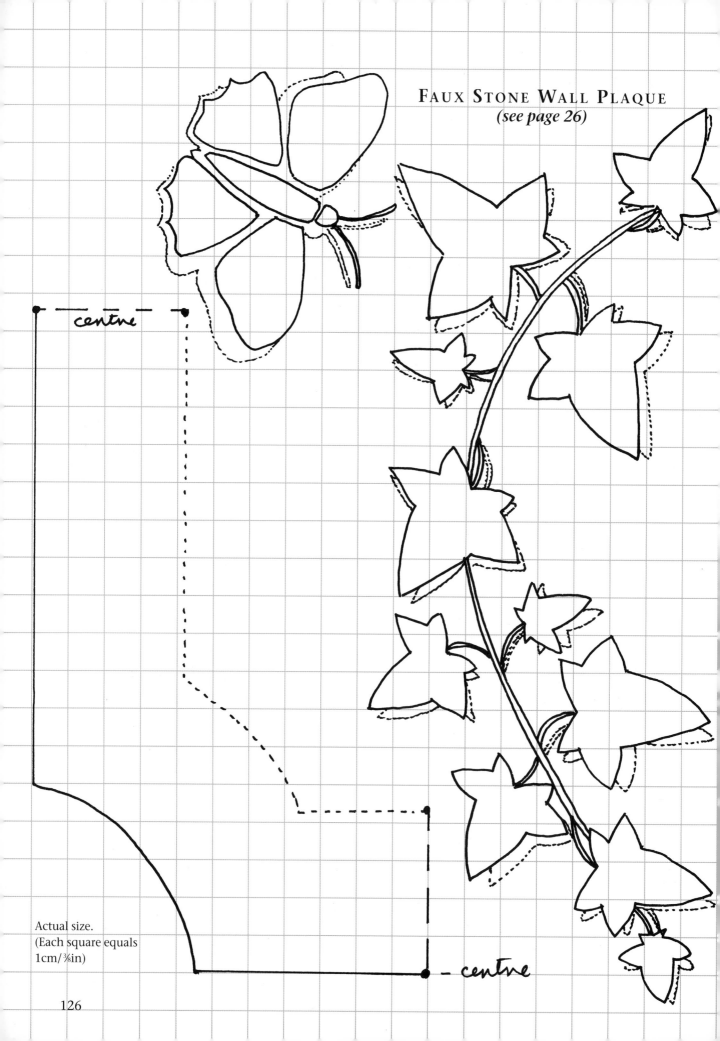

centre

centre

Actual size.
(Each square equals
1cm/⅜in)

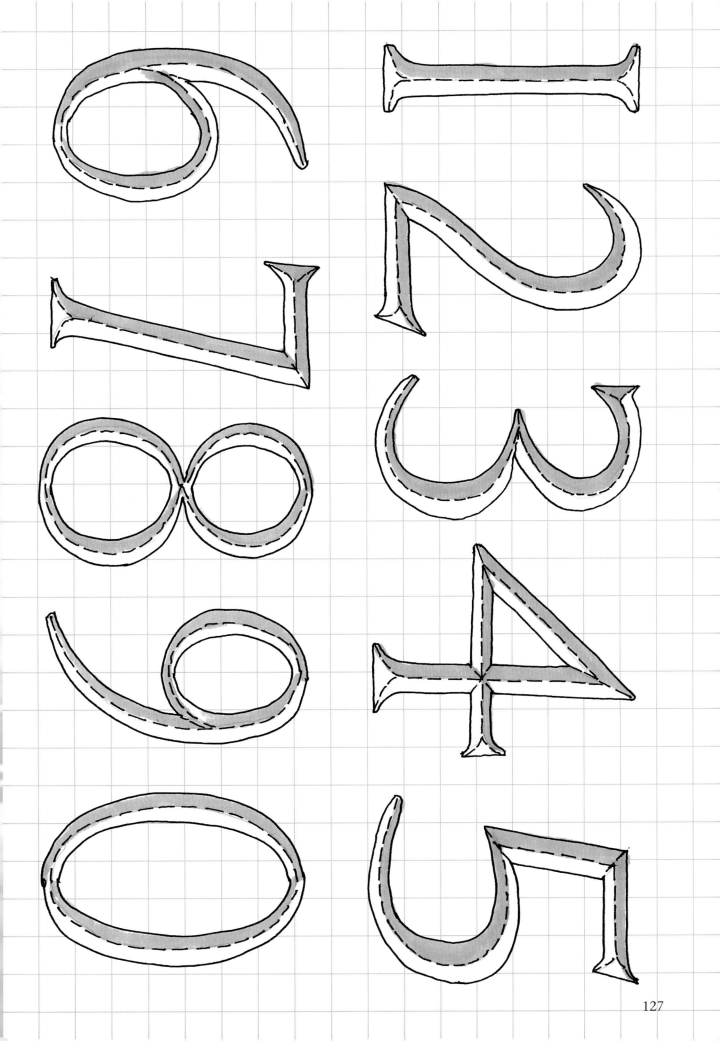

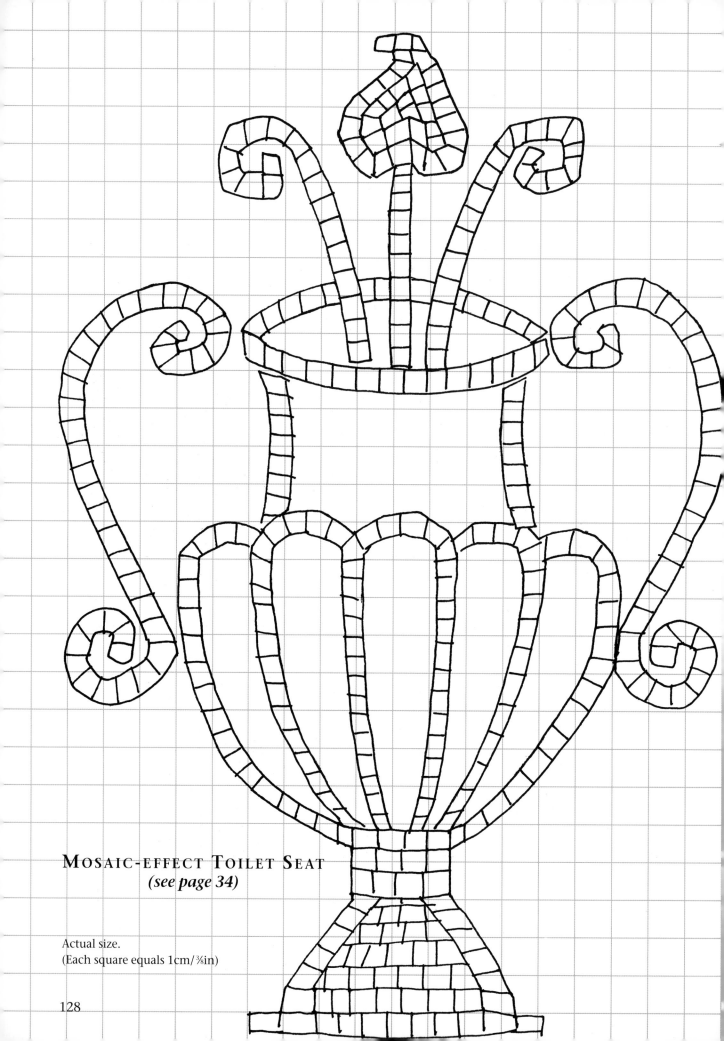

MOSAIC-EFFECT TOILET SEAT
(see page 34)

Actual size.
(Each square equals 1cm/⅜in)

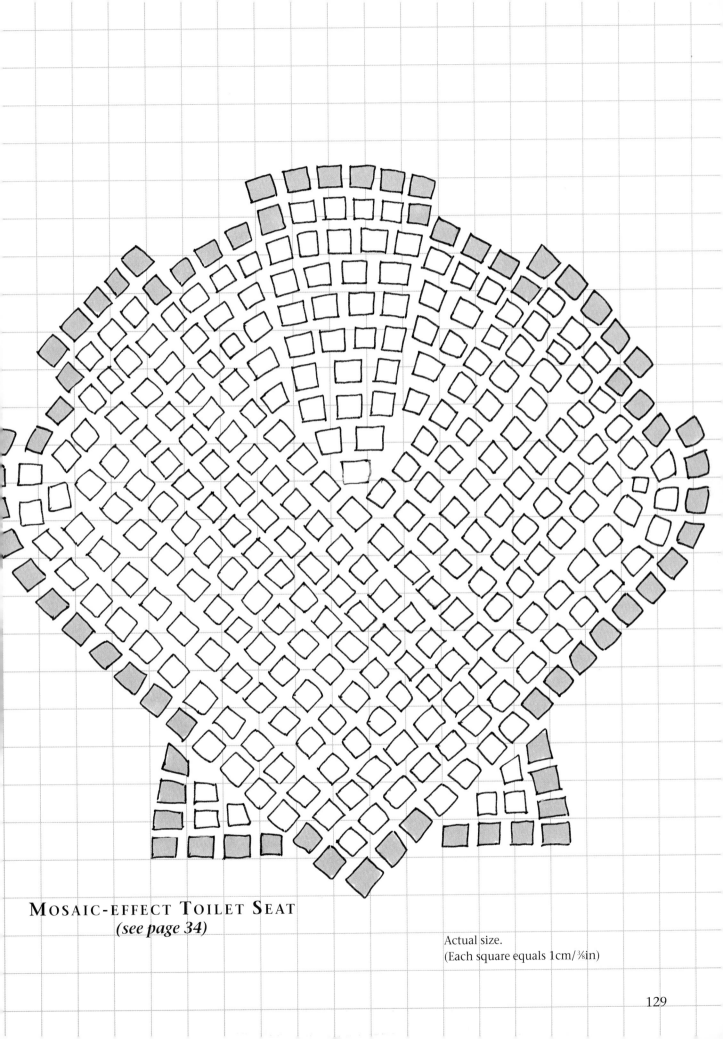

MOSAIC-EFFECT TOILET SEAT
(see page 34)

Actual size.
(Each square equals 1cm/⅜in)

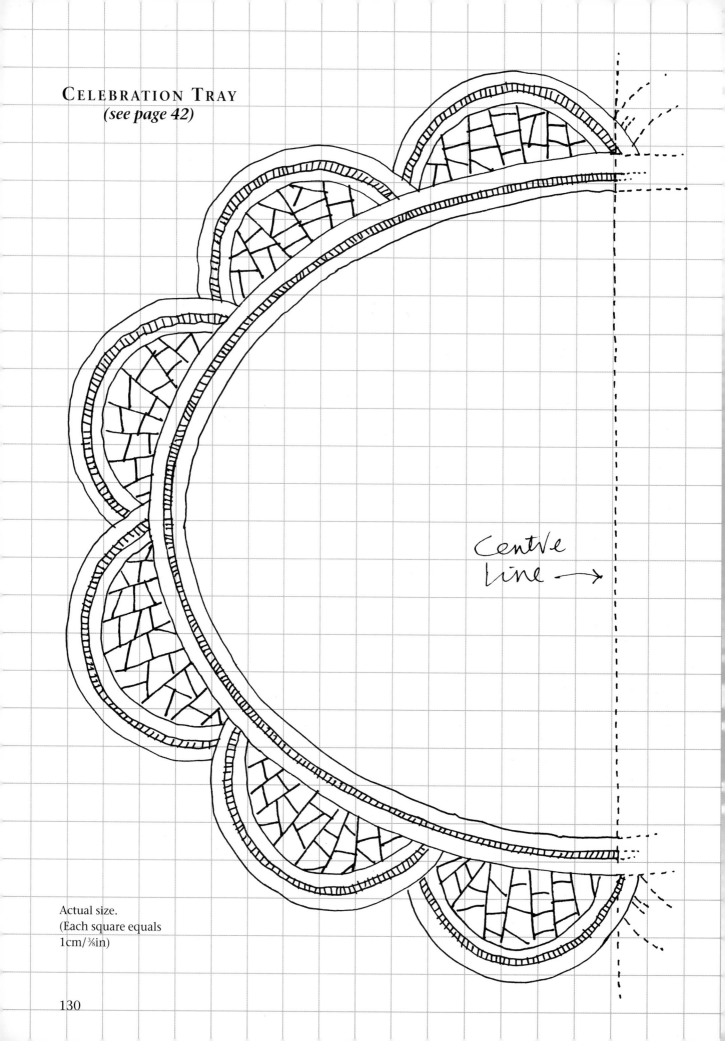

CELEBRATION TRAY
(see page 42)

Centre line →

Actual size.
(Each square equals
1cm/⅜in)

Actual size.
(Each square equals 1cm/⅜in)

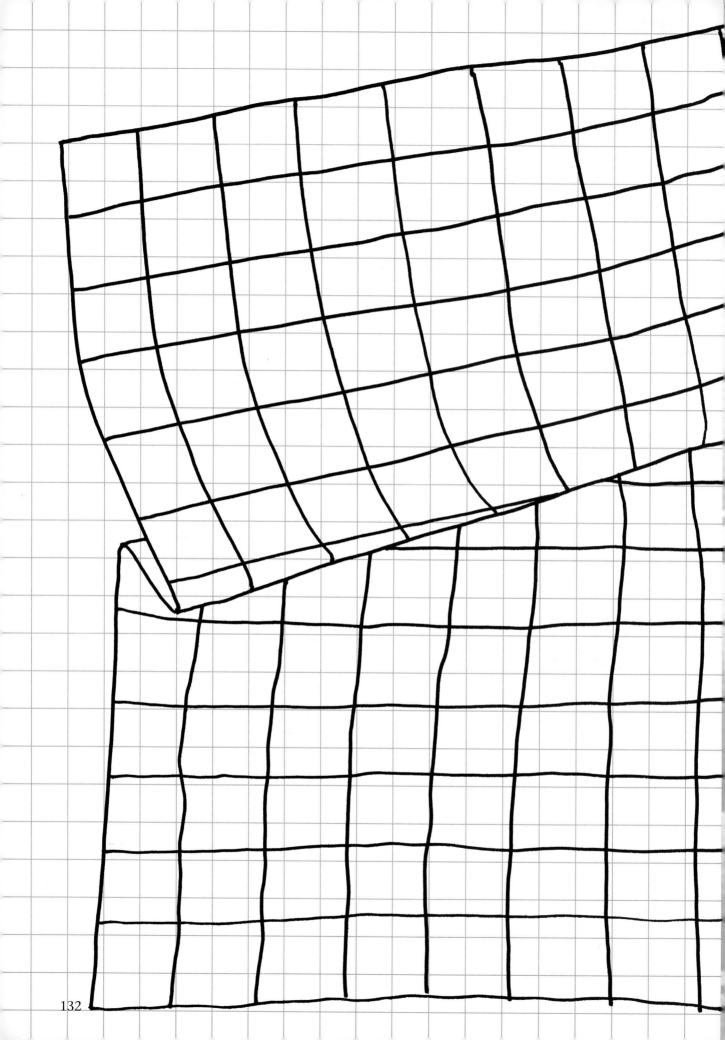

132

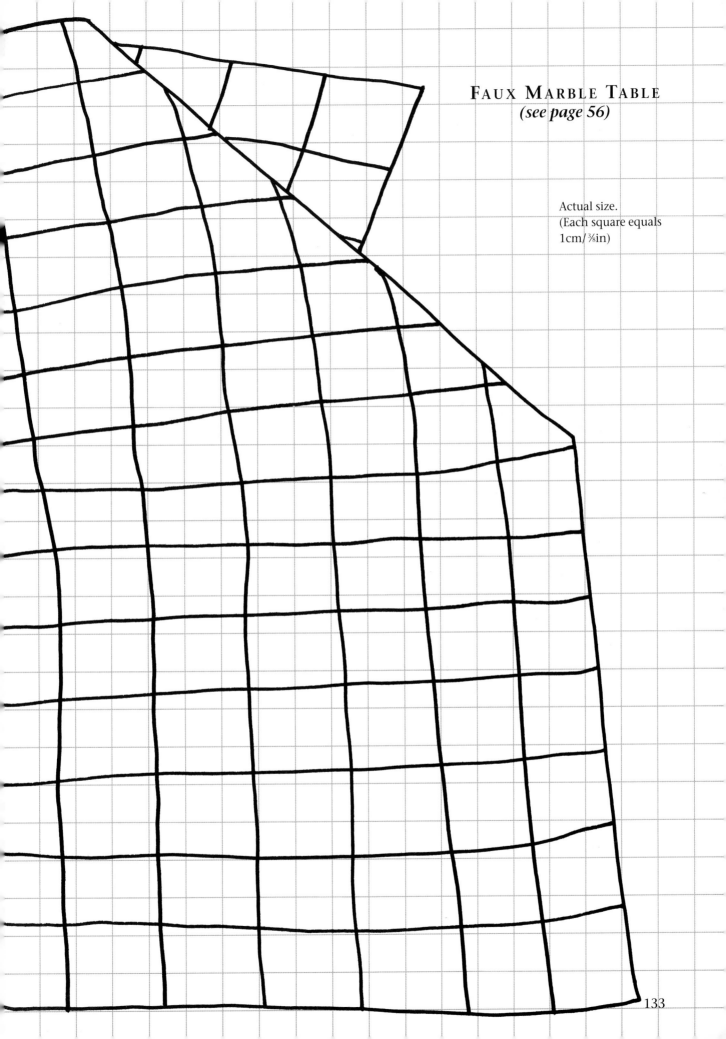

FAUX MARBLE TABLE
(see page 56)

Actual size.
(Each square equals
1cm/⅜in)

133

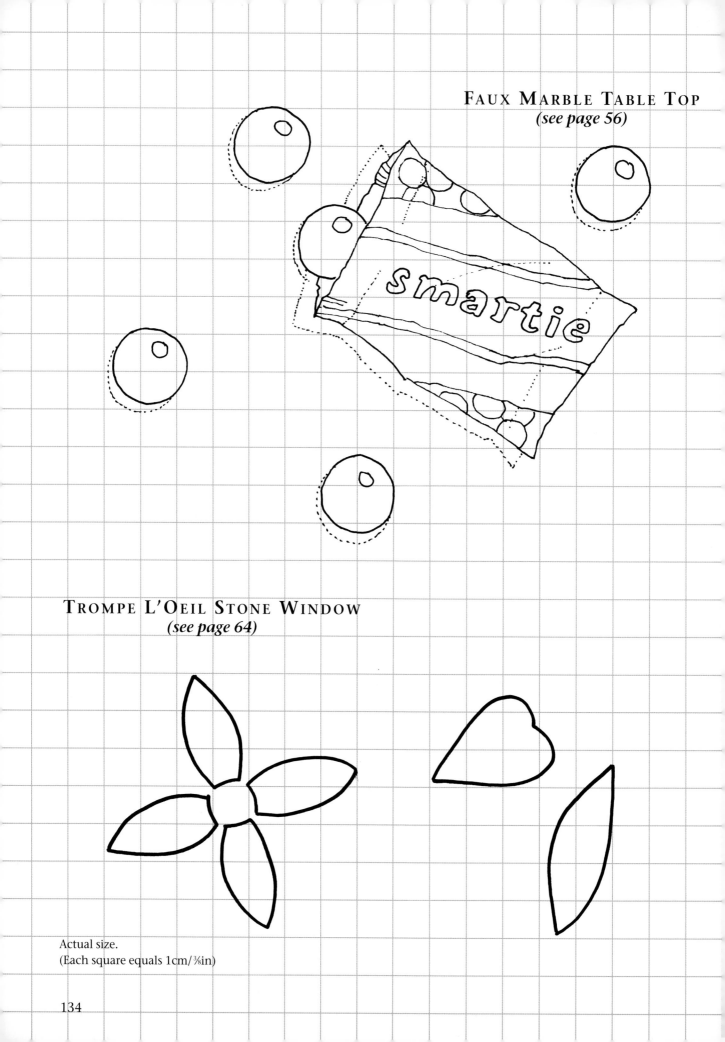

FAUX MARBLE TABLE TOP
(see page 56)

TROMPE L'OEIL STONE WINDOW
(see page 64)

Actual size.
(Each square equals 1cm/⅜in)

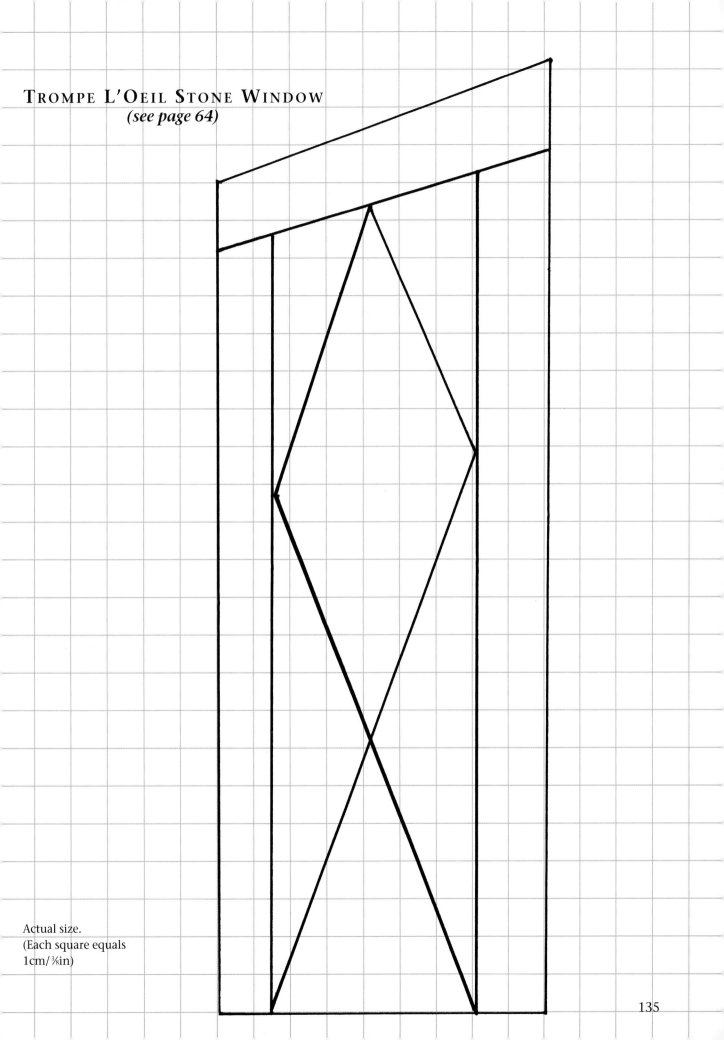

TROMPE L'OEIL STONE WINDOW
(see page 64)

Actual size.
(Each square equals
1cm/⅜in)

Memo Board
(see page 85)

Actual size.
(Each square equals 1cm/⅜in)

ABCDEFGHIJKLMN
OPQRSTUVWXYZ
abcdefghijklmnopqrstuvw
xyz&&& 1234567890!?

MEMO BOARD
(see page 80)

(Each square equals 1cm/⅜in)

A

B

Actual size.
(Each square equals 1cm/⅜in)

C

Actual size.
(Each square equals
1cm/⅜in)

D

ORIENTAL CUPBOARD
(see page 88)

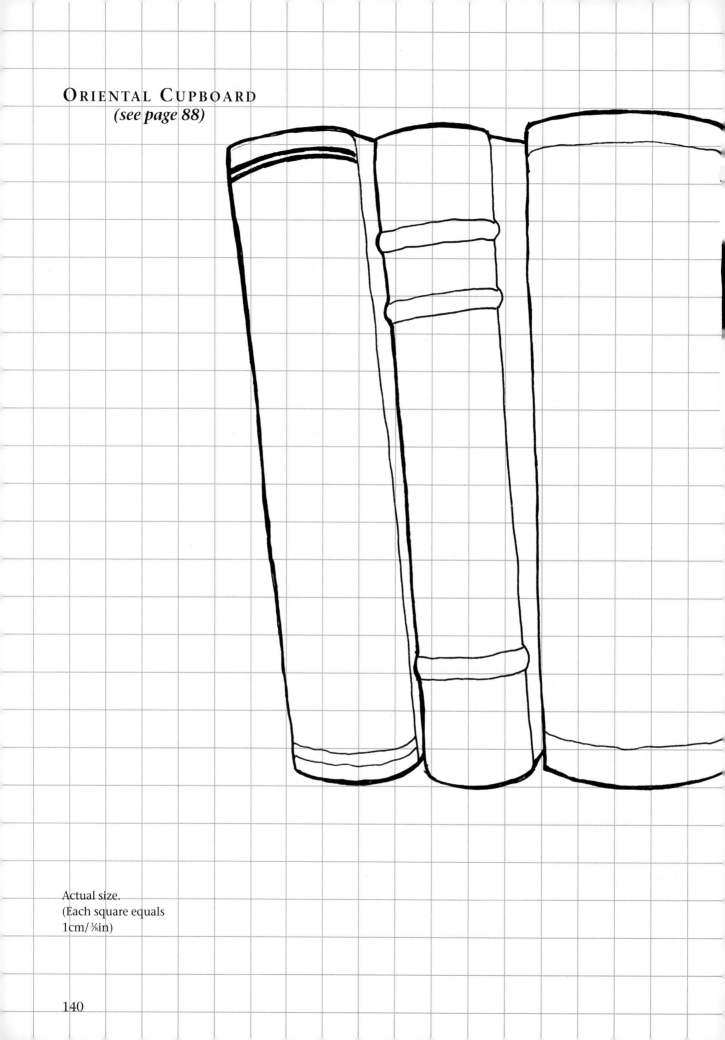

Actual size.
(Each square equals
1cm/⅜in)

ORIENTAL CUPBOARD
(see page 88)

Actual size.
(Each square equals 1cm/⅜in)

Trompe L'Oeil Fresco
(see page 98)

Each square equals 30cm (1ft). Enlarge to size.

Trompe L'Oeil Fresco
(see page 98)

Each square equals 30cm (1ft). Enlarge to size.

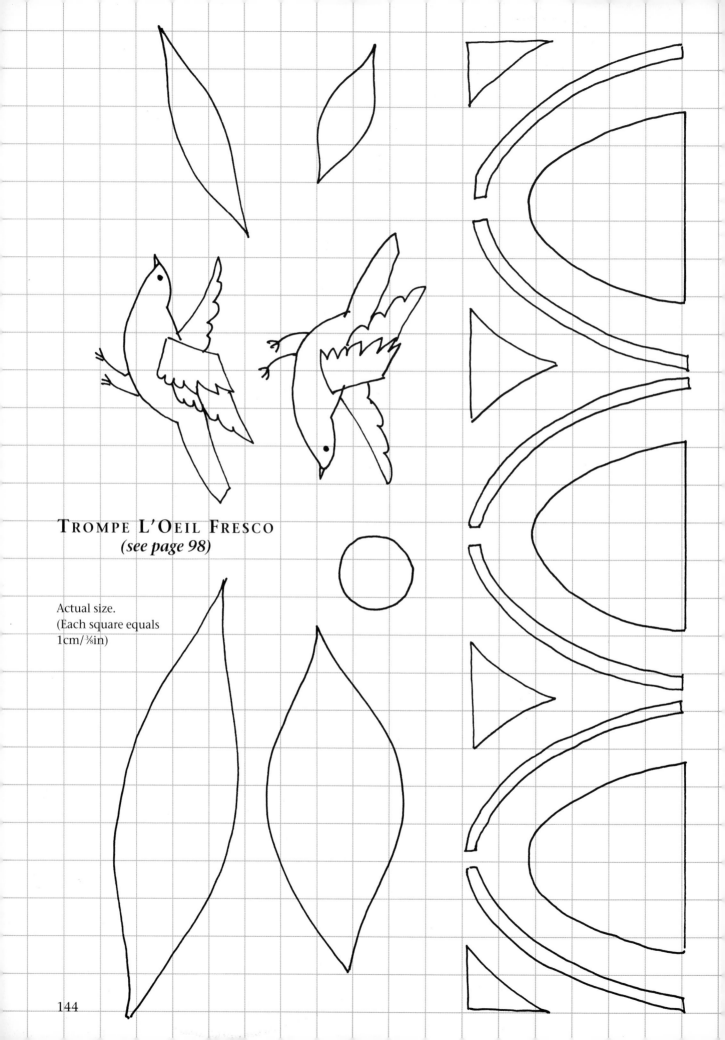

TROMPE L'OEIL FRESCO
(see page 98)

Actual size.
(Each square equals
1cm/⅜in)

Actual size.
(Each square equals
1cm/⅜in)

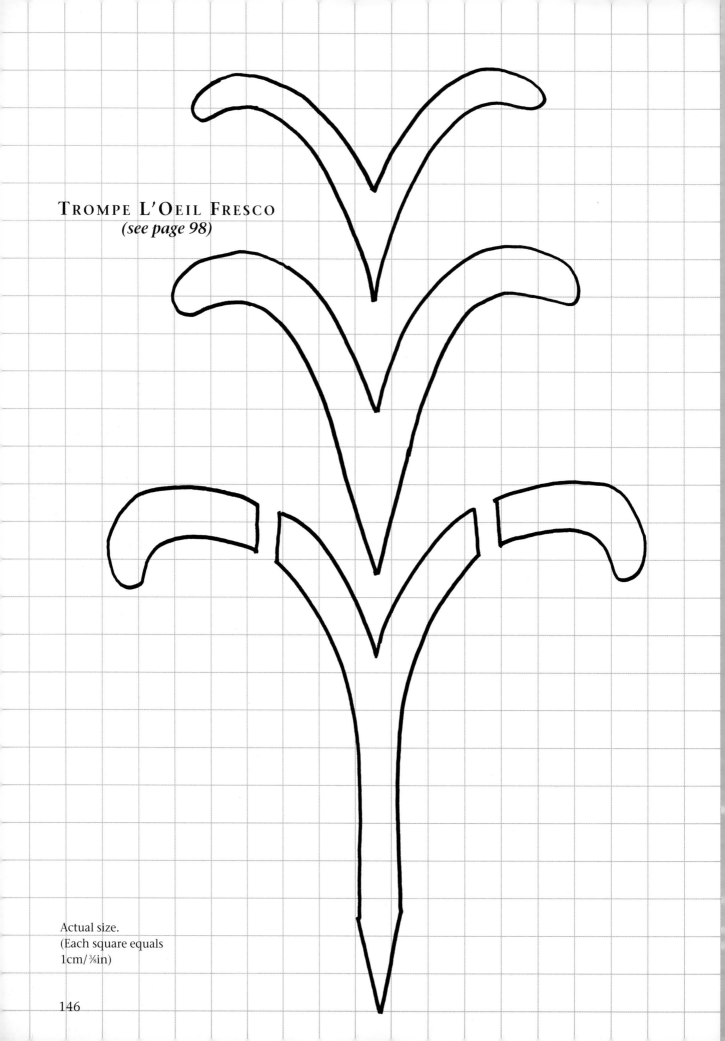

TROMPE L'OEIL FRESCO
(see page 98)

Actual size.
(Each square equals
1cm/⅜in)

MURAL DESIGN
(*see page 106*)

Actual size.
(Each square equals
1cm/⅜in)

Mural Design
(see page 106)

Enlarge to 38cm (15in).
(Each square equals
1cm/⅜in)

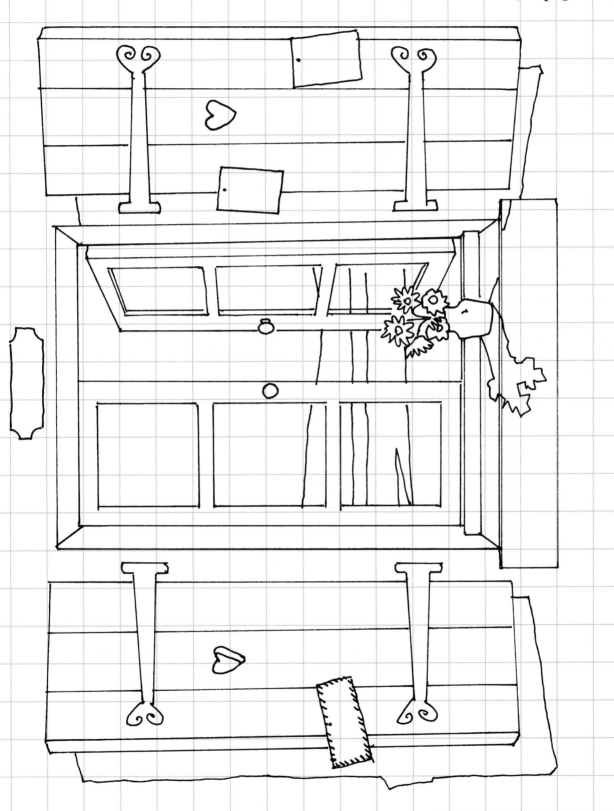

Each square equals 10cm (4in). Enlarge to 2.4m wide x 1.55m high (80 x 60in).

Detail of the mural around a stairwell on HMS Raleigh, showing the first official Royal Navy uniform (see 'About the Author', on page iii, for further information)

The author painting a section of scenery when she worked in the film industry

First official Officers uniform

1748

Faux marble sample board

INDEX

BOOKS

DOLLS' HOUSES AND MINIATURES

1/12 Scale Character Figures for the Dolls' House	*James Carrington*
Architecture for Dolls' Houses	*Joyce Percival*
The Authentic Georgian Dolls' House	*Brian Long*
A Beginners' Guide to the Dolls' House Hobby	*Jean Nisbett*
Celtic, Medieval and Tudor Wall Hangings in 1/12 Scale Needlepoint	*Sandra Whitehead*
The Complete Dolls' House Book	*Jean Nisbett*
The Dolls' House 1/24 Scale: A Complete Introduction	*Jean Nisbett*
Dolls' House Accessories, Fixtures and Fittings	*Andrea Barham*
Dolls' House Bathrooms: Lots of Little Loos	*Patricia King*
Dolls' House Fireplaces and Stoves	*Patricia King*
Dolls' House Window Treatments	*Eve Harwood*
Easy to Make Dolls' House Accessories	*Andrea Barham*
Heraldic Miniature Knights	*Peter Greenhill*
How to Make Your Dolls' House Special: Fresh Ideas for Decorating	*Beryl Armstrong*
Make Your Own Dolls' House Furniture	*Maurice Harper*
Making Dolls' House Furniture	*Patricia King*
Making Georgian Dolls' Houses	*Derek Rowbottom*
Making Miniature Food and Market Stalls	*Angie Scarr*
Making Miniature Gardens	*Freida Gray*
Making Miniature Oriental Rugs & Carpets	*Meik & Ian McNaughton*
Making Period Dolls' House Accessories	*Andrea Barham*
Making Tudor Dolls' Houses	*Derek Rowbottom*
Making Victorian Dolls' House Furniture	*Patricia King*
Miniature Bobbin Lace	*Roz Snowden*
Miniature Embroidery for the Georgian Dolls' House	*Pamela Warner*
Miniature Embroidery for the Victorian Dolls' House	*Pamela Warner*
Miniature Needlepoint Carpets	*Janet Granger*
More Miniature Oriental Rugs & Carpets	*Meik & Ian McNaughton*
Needlepoint 1/12 Scale: Design Collections for the Dolls' House	*Felicity Price*
The Secrets of the Dolls' House Makers	*Jean Nisbett*

CRAFTS

American Patchwork Designs in Needlepoint	*Melanie Tacon*
A Beginners' Guide to Rubber Stamping	*Brenda Hunt*
Blackwork: A New Approach	*Brenda Day*
Celtic Cross Stitch Designs	*Carol Phillipson*
Celtic Knotwork Designs	*Sheila Sturrock*
Celtic Knotwork Handbook	*Sheila Sturrock*
Celtic Spirals and Other Designs	*Sheila Sturrock*
Collage from Seeds, Leaves and Flowers	*Joan Carver*
Complete Pyrography	*Stephen Poole*
Contemporary Smocking	*Dorothea Hall*
Creating Colour with Dylon	*Dylon International*
Creative Doughcraft	*Patricia Hughes*
Creative Embroidery Techniques Using Colour Through Gold	*Daphne J. Ashby & Jackie Woolsey*
The Creative Quilter: Techniques and Projects	*Pauline Brown*
Decorative Beaded Purses	*Enid Taylor*
Designing and Making Cards	*Glennis Gilruth*
Glass Engraving Pattern Book	*John Everett*
Glass Painting	*Emma Sedman*
Handcrafted Rugs	*Sandra Hardy*
How to Arrange Flowers: A Japanese Approach to English Design	*Taeko Marvelly*

How to Make First-Class Cards	*Debbie Brown*
An Introduction to Crewel Embroidery	*Mave Glenny*
Making and Using Working Drawings for Realistic Model Animals	*Basil F. Fordham*
Making Character Bears	*Valerie Tyler*
Making Decorative Screens	*Amanda Howes*
Making Fairies and Fantastical Creatures	*Julie Sharp*
Making Greetings Cards for Beginners	*Pat Sutherland*
Making Hand-Sewn Boxes: Techniques and Projects	*Jackie Woolsey*
Making Knitwear Fit	*Pat Ashforth & Steve Plummer*
Making Mini Cards, Gift Tags & Invitations	*Glennis Gilruth*
Making Soft-Bodied Dough Characters	*Patricia Hughes*
Natural Ideas for Christmas: Fantastic Decorations to Make	*Josie Cameron-Ashcroft & Carol Cox*
Needlepoint: A Foundation Course	*Sandra Hardy*
New Ideas for Crochet: Stylish Projects for the Home	*Darsha Capaldi*
Patchwork for Beginners	*Pauline Brown*
Pyrography Designs	*Norma Gregory*
Pyrography Handbook (Practical Crafts)	*Stephen Poole*
Ribbons and Roses	*Lee Lockheed*
Rose Windows for Quilters	*Angela Besley*
Rubber Stamping with Other Crafts	*Lynne Garner*
Sponge Painting	*Ann Rooney*
Stained Glass: Techniques and Projects	*Mary Shanahan*
Step-by-Step Pyrography Projects for the Solid Point Machine	*Norma Gregory*
Tassel Making for Beginners	*Enid Taylor*
Tatting Collage	*Lindsay Rogers*
Temari: A Traditional Japanese Embroidery Technique	*Margaret Ludlow*
Theatre Models in Paper and Card	*Robert Burgess*
Trip Around the World: 25 Patchwork, Quilting and Appliqué Projects	*Gail Lawther*
Trompe L'Oeil: Techniques and Projects	*Jan Lee Johnson*
Wool Embroidery and Design	*Lee Lockheed*

MAGAZINES

WOODTURNING ◆ WOODCARVING ◆ FURNITURE & CABINETMAKING
THE ROUTER ◆ WOODWORKING ◆ THE DOLLS' HOUSE MAGAZINE
WATER GARDENING ◆ EXOTIC GARDENING ◆ GARDEN CALENDAR
OUTDOOR PHOTOGRAPHY ◆ BLACK & WHITE PHOTOGRAPHY
BUSINESSMATTERS

The above represents a selection of the titles currently published or scheduled to be published. All are available direct from the Publishers or through bookshops, newsagents and specialist retailers. To place an order, or to obtain a complete catalogue, contact:

GMC Publications,
Castle Place, 166 High Street, Lewes,
East Sussex BN7 1XU, United Kingdom
Tel: 01273 488005 Fax: 01273 478606
E-mail: pubs@thegmcgroup.com

Orders by credit card are accepted